THE OFFICIAL **BBC**SPORT GUIDE

FORMULA ONE 2015

This edition published in 2015
by Carlton Books Limited
20 Mortimer Street
London W1T 3JW

ISBN: 978-1-78097-607-5

Design Direction: Luke Griffin
Designer: Ben Ruocco
Production: Maria Petalidou
Picture Research: Paul Langan
Editorial: Conor Kilgallon and Caroline Curtis
Project Editor: Matthew Lowing

Printed in Spain

Opposite: Formula One grands prix aren't always run in the sun.

THE OFFICIAL BBC SPORT GUIDE
FORMULA ONE 2015

BRUCE JONES

CARLTON
BOOKS

CONTENTS

4

Right: The Marina Bay circuit in downtown Singapore provides a spectacular setting to go racing – and holding its race after dark adds to the show.

No circuit adds colour and passion to its grand prix as much as the Italian GP. Should Ferrari win, then the Tifosi go wild. In 2014, Lewis Hamilton triumphed, followed by team-mate Nico Rosberg and Williams' Felipe Massa.

ANALYSIS OF THE 2015 SEASON

Last year was a sea change in F1 with the introduction of a host of new technical rules. Mercedes stole a march and the big question is whether any of the rival teams can fight back. Williams took a huge leap forward and Red Bull Racing fought back. However, most eyes will be on McLaren, which welcomes not only Fernando Alonso but all-new Honda engines and hopes to emulate their previous successes together.

Going into the 2014 World Championship, off the back of four straight titles for Red Bull Racing, people hoped that there would be a change at the top. You wonder whether those same people who seek variety are already hoping that Mercedes can be toppled, such was the team's dominance last year.

There has been no change in the technical regulations for 2015 and the team continued to develop its car through last season, maintaining its initial advantage, so there's no reason at all why Lewis Hamilton and Nico Rosberg won't expect to go for gold again.

Red Bull Racing knows that Renault will have had to do something special to get its V6 turbo to match Mercedes' equivalent and this was what held the team back last year. If they can't make the advances in terms of power and usability in the close-season, they will no doubt be canvassing again for the engine freeze being lifted during the season too, as they tried to do last year unsuccessfully. Daniel Ricciardo was excellent in his first year with a front-line team, taking the three wins that escaped Mercedes' drivers, and he is being joined by 2014 rookie Daniil Kvyat, who excelled with Scuderia Toro Rosso.

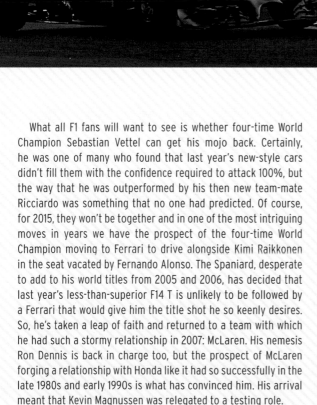

What all F1 fans will want to see is whether four-time World Champion Sebastian Vettel can get his mojo back. Certainly, he was one of many who found that last year's new-style cars didn't fill them with the confidence required to attack 100%, but the way that he was outperformed by his then new team-mate Ricciardo was something that no one had predicted. Of course, for 2015, they won't be together and in one of the most intriguing moves in years we have the prospect of the four-time World Champion moving to Ferrari to drive alongside Kimi Raikkonen in the seat vacated by Fernando Alonso. The Spaniard, desperate to add to his world titles from 2005 and 2006, has decided that last year's less-than-superior F14 T is unlikely to be followed by a Ferrari that would give him the title shot he so keenly desires. So, he's taken a leap of faith and returned to a team with which he had such a stormy relationship in 2007: McLaren. His nemesis Ron Dennis is back in charge too, but the prospect of McLaren forging a relationship with Honda like it had so successfully in the late 1980s and early 1990s is what has convinced him. His arrival meant that Kevin Magnussen was relegated to a testing role.

Williams has stuck with the same line-up of Valtteri Bottas, Felipe Massa and, importantly, Mercedes engines. The successful turnaround of its technical side, guided by Pat Symonds, really bore fruit last year and offers every chance of the team continuing to shoot for podium results and, who knows, even victories.

Having spent much of last year ahead of McLaren, Force India boosted its reputation and it sticks with the pairing of Nico Hulkenberg and the more mercurial Sergio Perez.

Toro Rosso will make history at the Australian GP when its new signing Max Verstappen will become F1's youngest racer, at 17 years and 166 days. As rapid as he has proved in his one year of car racing since stepping up from karts, he'll have to make do with a rookie team-mate, Carlos Sainz Jr, so won't have experience to guide him.

Romain Grosjean and Pastor Maldonado deserve a better car beneath them than Lotus provided last year – and will surely get one. Better still, a deal to swap from Renault engines to Mercedes is sure to give them extra hope of becoming regular point scorers.

Sauber will be desperate to score points this year after its points-free campaign in 2014. Marcus Ericsson has arrived from Caterham and Felipe Nasr brings welcome backing from Brazil, but the team has lost continuity in changing both drivers in one go. However, as its financial situation was so meagre last year while both Marussia and Caterham teetered on the edge of closing, it's understandable why the deals were done.

Fans became nervous last year in the run-up to the double-points final round, worried that it could affect the outcome in a way that they didn't like. They can relax this year because it has been confined to history as an experiment that proved less than popular.

MERCEDES AMG PETRONAS

Mercedes turned itself into the team to beat in 2014, adapting to the new rules much better than its rivals and dominating the show. All it can hope to improve upon this year is the relationship between its drivers, Lewis Hamilton and Nico Rosberg.

We must hope that the Mercedes team bosses continue to allow Nico Rosberg and Lewis Hamilton to fight unfettered for glory in 2015.

Having established itself at the top of the F1 pile in 2014, Mercedes GP is now the team to beat, but it's a team that has had more than a few identities. Having taken over Tyrrell's championship entry in 1998, it started afresh the following year when it burst onto the scene with almost unprecedented fanfare as BAR, proclaiming itself to have "a tradition of excellence". Sure, the team arrived with considerable backing from a global tobacco giant (racing as British American Racing), it had an impressive new headquarters at Brackley and it had headhunted its staff from up and down the pitlane, but it had never entered a race. People almost waited to watch this brash newcomer stumble.

Headed by Jacques Villeneuve's manager Craig Pollock, BAR ran Villeneuve and Ricardo Zonta in that first year, and its finishing record was awful. Villeneuve must have wished that he'd stayed at Williams. Yet, in time, BAR began to move forwards when it swapped Mecachrome engines for Honda units for its second year and started to score points more than occasionally.

Pollock moved on and Prodrive boss David Richards came in to take control in 2002, and by the following year the team began to look more solid: Jenson Button had arrived and he now outshone Villeneuve, helping BAR to rank fifth.

THE POWER AND THE GLORY

PADDY LOWE
Here is a man of intellect who spent his early years at Williams, making its active suspension the class of the field in Nigel Mansell's title year, 1992. Moving to McLaren in 1993, he worked on the invisible developments such as power steering and brake steer. In time, he appeared at races and rose to become technical director before leaving the team during 2013. Since joining Mercedes, Paddy assumed a similar position following Bob Bell's departure.

TAKING CONTROL AFTER RULE CHANGE
Last year was a gilded but fractious year as Mercedes emerged with both titles but also an image besmirched by the scrapping between its drivers. Nico Rosberg won the opener in Melbourne, and it was apparent that the team's package was a good one. Lewis Hamilton then won the next four before their spat started at Monaco. When Rosberg clipped Hamilton at Spa, the conflict boiled over. However, things settled down and Hamilton went on to become the drivers' champion long after the team had secured the constructors' crown.

2014 DRIVERS & RESULTS

Driver	Nationality	Races	Wins	Pts	Pos
Lewis Hamilton	British	19	11	384	1st
Nico Rosberg	German	19	5	317	2nd

FOR THE RECORD

Country of origin:	England
Team base:	Brackley, England
Telephone:	(44) 01280 844000
Website:	www.mercedes-amg-f1.com
Active in Formula One:	As BAR 1999-2005; Honda Racing 2006-08; Brawn GP 2009
Grands Prix contested:	284
Wins:	29
Pole positions:	35
Fastest laps:	19

THE TEAM

Non-executive chairman:	Niki Lauda
Head of Mercedes-Benz Motorsport:	Toto Wolff
Executive director, technical:	Paddy Lowe
MD, Mercedes-Benz AMG High Performance powertrains:	Andy Cowell
Technology director:	Geoff Willis
Engineering director:	Aldo Costa
Performance director:	Mark Ellis
Chief designer:	John Owen
Chief race engineer:	Andrew Shovlin
Chief track engineer:	Simon Cole
Sporting director:	Ron Meadows
Test driver:	Pascal Wehrlein
Chassis:	Mercedes F1 W06
Engine:	Mercedes V6
Tyres:	Pirelli

Then in 2004 Button was able to take it to Ferrari's Michael Schumacher, finishing on the podium 10 times though never winning, and the team proved to be best of the rest behind Ferrari. The following year was less of a success.

For 2006, the team was rebranded as Honda Racing and its day of days came at the Hungaroring when Button read the mixed conditions better than anyone to score both his and the team's first win. He and Rubens Barrichello then had a shock in 2007, when the team failed to manage the change from Michelin to Bridgestone tyres well and seldom scored. It didn't improve in 2008 and its lack of results, combined with the global economic crash, led to Honda's withdrawal.

A desperate scramble ensued before Ross Brawn was able to save the team, helped by some finance from Honda. The result was something beyond his wildest dreams. Keeping on Button and Barrichello as his drivers, he presented them with a golden opportunity to revive their careers because the design team had come up with a double diffuser concept that was to propel its cars to the very front. Button won six times to become World Champion and Barrichello's two wins helped the team

win the constructors' championship too.

For 2010, the team was taken over by Mercedes and the cars turned out in the silver livery that Mercedes had used in its 1930s heyday and then again in its brief return in 1954 and 1955. Showing its clout, Mercedes coaxed seven-time World Champion Michael Schumacher out of retirement. There must have been hopes that the wins would continue, but no more technical advantages were discovered, and the next win came only in 2012, Mercedes' third year back, when Nico Rosberg was triumphant at the Chinese GP.

Lewis Hamilton replaced Schumacher in 2013 and the team pipped Ferrari to rank second overall behind Red Bull Racing, thanks to the English driver's win at the Hungaroring and Rosberg's pair at Monaco and Silverstone. Then came its 2014 glories.

For 2015, it's vital that Mercedes makes its drivers behave and go out to race for the team, and not just for themselves.

With the team's key personnel all staying on, there's no reason why Mercedes won't remain at the top.

"You can't take anything for granted over the winter in F1. We just have to do our best and see where we are when we turn up for 2015."
Paddy Lowe

Rosberg and Hamilton had plenty to celebrate in 2014. Will they still be smiling this year?

LEWIS HAMILTON

Last year showed Lewis back to his very best, racing with the sheer passion that marked out his early career, his personal distractions things of the past. For 2015, nothing less than a third world title will do.

Lewis's father worked night and day to put Lewis through karting. Famously, the pivotal moment came when Lewis asked McLaren boss Ron Dennis to back him. Lewis was 11 and Dennis logged the moment. Two years later, he went for it and the rest is history: Lewis used that backing well to win a series of karting titles, culminating in the World Kart Cup in 2000.

Lewis dipped his toe in the car-racing pond with the British Formula Renault winter series at the end of 2001. He became a race winner in 2002, then British champion in 2003. Formula 3 was next and Lewis won the European F3 title at his second attempt, beating Adrian Sutil and Sebastian Vettel. GP2 was a challenge that he won at his first attempt, in 2006.

Then, unusually for a rookie, he was given his F1 break by a top team: McLaren. The team's other signing was Fernando Alonso, which meant that this would be a learning year, but Lewis was soon indignant if he hadn't got a crack at winning. He took that breakthrough victory in Canada and could easily have landed the title but for stumbles in the last two rounds. Twelve months later, at Interlagos, he prevailed

Lewis rediscovered his mojo in 2014 and his 11 wins and second F1 title were just reward.

after a battle with Ferrari's Felipe Massa.

Since then, Lewis has always been a challenger but he became frustrated that McLaren had no answer to Red Bull Racing. He quit McLaren for Mercedes for 2013 and raced alongside former karting team-mate Nico Rosberg, ending the year fourth overall to Rosberg's sixth.

TRACK NOTES

Nationality:	BRITISH
Born:	7 JANUARY 1985, STEVENAGE, ENGLAND
Website:	www.lewishamilton.com
Teams:	McLAREN 2007-12, MERCEDES 2013-15

CAREER RECORD

First Grand Prix:	2007 AUSTRALIAN GP
Grand Prix starts:	148
Grand Prix wins:	33

2007 Canadian GP, United States GP, Hungarian GP, Japanese GP, 2008 Australian GP, Monaco GP, British GP, German GP, Chinese GP, 2009 Hungarian GP, Singapore GP, 2010 Turkish GP, Canadian GP, Belgian GP, 2011 Chinese GP, German GP, Abu Dhabi GP, 2012 Canadian GP, Hungarian GP, Italian GP, United States GP, 2013 Hungarian GP, 2014 Malaysian GP, Bahrain GP, Chinese GP, Spanish GP, British GP, Italian GP, Singapore GP, Japanese GP, Russian GP, United States GP, Abu Dhabi GP

Poles:	38
Fastest laps:	20
Points:	1486

Honours: 2014 FORMULA ONE WORLD CHAMPION, 2008 FORMULA ONE WORLD CHAMPION, 2007 RUNNER-UP, 2006 GP2 CHAMPION, 2005 EUROPEAN FORMULA THREE CHAMPION, 2003 BRITISH FORMULA RENAULT CHAMPION, 2000 WORLD KART CUP CHAMPION & EUROPEAN FORMULA A KART CHAMPION, 1999 ITALIAN INTERCONTINENTAL A KART CHAMPION, 1996 McLAREN MERCEDES CHAMPION OF THE FUTURE

RACING FOR WINS AND TITLES

Lewis has had some up and down seasons, so it was good that he largely let his driving do the talking in 2014. Displaying a degree more maturity, he overcame his various spats with Mercedes team-mate Nico Rosberg to start delivering some stunning, race-winning drives. He also rose above and even profited from occasions that would previously have sent him into a tailspin, such as when he backed off in final qualifying at a wet but drying Silverstone and threw away pole position. Frustrated by mechanical failure in the season-opening race in Melbourne, Lewis then rode the wave of Mercedes' form to win the next four races. Yet, with only Rosberg as a title rival, he was still just three points clear. All that could hurt either of the rivals was a race retirement, and mechanical woes hit both of them. The way that Lewis dealt with the second half of the year must have given him the most pleasure as he hunted Rosberg down.

NICO ROSBERG

Last year was by far Nico's best yet in F1 as he seized the opportunity of driving the best car in the field for the first time in his career in the World Championship, and grabbed poles and wins to take the title battle right to the end of the season.

When Nico's father Keke scaled racing's ladder to reach F1, he did it by racing anything, anywhere. He wasn't afraid to commute back and forth across the Atlantic Ocean and run multiple programmes, determined to do anything to advance to the next level. Once he'd made it to F1, he was able to show his raw speed to those who hadn't noticed before, his victory in the International Trophy in an unfancied Theodore in 1978 proving to be his calling card. Seen as the fastest of the fast and the bravest of the brave, he joined Williams and won the 1982 drivers' title.

For Nico, the path was not so rocky because Keke financed his climb through karting. Runner-up to Lewis Hamilton in the 2000 European Formula A kart series, Nico moved on to car racing in 2002 when he was still 16. Racing in the Formula BMW ADAC Championship, he dominated, earning his graduation to F3 for 2003. Eighth overall that year, he came back for a second season in the European Championship, but could rank only fourth, albeit one place ahead of Hamilton. Nonetheless, it was felt that Nico was ready for GP2 and he joined the crack ART Grand Prix team, claiming five wins to

Nico rose to new heights in 2014, especially in qualifying, and will come back stronger still.

beat Heikki Kovalainen to the title at his first attempt.

Thus it was that Nico became the latest second-generation F1 racer, landing a ride with father's old team, Williams, for 2006. Setting fastest lap on his F1 debut

in Bahrain was a great start, but the team became gradually less competitive and it was with a sigh of relief that he signed for Mercedes for 2010, only to discover that his new team-mate would be the returning Michael Schumacher. To his credit, Nico proved faster than his appreciably older compatriot and gave the team its first win at Shanghai in 2012 and then added two more in 2013.

Then came his sternest challenge in 2014 and he rose to new heights.

TRACK NOTES

Nationality:	GERMAN
Born:	27 JUNE 1985, WIESBADEN, GERMANY
Website:	www.nicorosberg.com
Teams:	WILLIAMS 2006-09, MERCEDES 2010-15

CAREER RECORD

First Grand Prix:	2006 BAHRAIN GP
Grand Prix starts:	166
Grand Prix wins:	8
2012 Chinese GP, 2013 Monaco GP, British GP, 2014 Australian GP, Monaco GP, Austrian GP, German GP, Brazilian GP	
Poles:	15
Fastest laps:	9
Points:	887.5
Honours:	2014 FORMULA ONE WORLD RUNNER-UP, 2005 GP2 CHAMPION, 2003 EUROPEAN FORMULA THREE ROOKIE RUNNER-UP, 2002 FORMULA BMW ADAC CHAMPION, 2000 EUROPEAN FORMULA A KART RUNNER-UP

BECOMING A REGULAR WINNER

One win for Mercedes in 2012 and two in 2013 were hints of what this second-generation racer could deliver. Armed with the most competitive car in the field last year, Nico really took the title battle to his more highly ranked team-mate Lewis Hamilton. Not only did he deliver winning performances, starting off at the season-opener in Melbourne, he would also finish second on those occasions when he didn't win. Thus he put Hamilton under pressure. He added to it other ways, showing a new-found determination that was less than sporting: refusing to be intimidated, he ensured that Hamilton didn't complete his final qualifying run at Monaco and then intentionally left his wheel in the way during their tussle at the Belgian GP. This required a reading of the riot act by Mercedes, which didn't want its dominance producing only a clash between its own drivers. Eventually, after a few retirements struck his car, Nico found himself on the back foot, but the fight went on.

Precision is everything in pitstops, and this aerial shot of a Lewis Hamilton pit visit is poetry in infinitely orchestrated motion.

RED BULL RACING

After years of coming out on top – sometimes by a lot, other times by a little –
Red Bull Racing was less than the best in 2014 and now hopes that a boost from
engine supplier Renault can move it back to the front, led by Daniel Ricciardo.

Daniel Ricciardo was the revelation of last season, mastering not only the Red Bull RB10 but his much-titled team-mate Sebastian Vettel.

Four years of one team coming out on top in the World Championship, with Sebastian Vettel champion each time, meant that fans were glad of the change last year when Mercedes took over as the dominant team.

And yet, only a few years ago, this was a team that couldn't win – for love nor money. It began life in 1997 as Stewart GP. Founded by triple world champion Jackie Stewart and his elder son Paul, this was a step up from its F3000 team and was built on a firm base. The white and tartan-liveried cars' results improved through 1998 and the team scored a surprise one-three finish in the 1999 European GP at the Nürburgring, with Johnny Herbert winning and Rubens Barrichello two places behind.

For 2001, there was a change of ownership, as the Stewarts sold the team to Ford. The automotive giant then entered the cars in a green livery and branded it as Jaguar Racing, with great hopes of taking on the top teams. Yet, despite the cash injection, it remained stolidly in the midfield despite the often excellent endeavours of first Eddie Irvine and then Mark Webber.

In 2005, the team was rebranded again when Dietrich Mateschitz used his millions from the Red Bull energy drink to buy the team. Webber didn't stay on but would rejoin in 2007, by which time Adrian Newey's first Red Bull chassis was on stream. Both

THE POWER AND THE GLORY

DIETRICH MATESCHITZ
Before Dietrich Mateschitz came along, no F1 sponsor had ever formed a team good enough to win a grand prix. The 70-year-old Austrian energy drinks magnate has exceeded that by far. In his wish for Red Bull to be associated with adrenaline sports, he now owns two F1 teams – Scuderia Toro Rosso is the second – and his money has bought the right people for Red Bull Racing to land four constructors' and four drivers' titles.

LEARNING TO LIVE LIFE AS A CHASER
Red Bull Racing was a shadow of its former self in 2014. If it won races, this was usually because Mercedes had tripped up. Not only did its cars lack pace-setting performance, but their reliability was poor. Much of this was due to its new turbocharged Renault V6 engines, though some blame could be placed upon Newey's design team for being too aggressive in its packaging, leading to overheating. New signing Ricciardo was a revelation, racking up wins while Vettel didn't – a situation that none had forseen.

2014 DRIVERS & RESULTS

Driver	Nationality	Races	Wins	Pts	Pos
Daniel Ricciardo	Australian	19	3	238	3rd
Sebastian Vettel	German	19	0	167	5th

FOR THE RECORD

Country of origin:	England
Team base:	Milton Keynes, England
Telephone:	(44) 01908 279700
Website:	www.infiniti-redbullracing.com
Active in Formula One:	As Stewart GP
	1997-2000; Jaguar Racing 2001-2004
Grands Prix contested:	319
Wins:	51
Pole positions:	58
Fastest laps:	44

THE TEAM

Chairman:	Dietrich Mateschitz
Team principal:	Christian Horner
Chief technical officer:	Adrian Newey
Chief designer:	Rob Marshall
Head of aerodynamics:	Dan Fallows
Chief engineer, car engineering:	Paul Monaghan
Chief engineer, performance engineering:	Pierre Wache
Head of electronics:	Paul Everington
Team manager:	Joanathan Wheatley
Test driver:	Sebastien Buemi
Chassis:	Red Bull RB11
Engine:	Renault V6
Tyres:	Pirelli

he and David Coulthard (who had coaxed Newey to join from McLaren) benefited as the results improved. The team's move to the big time came in 2009, when both new signing Sebastian Vettel and Webber won races as they ranked second and fourth respectively, the team finishing the year as runner-up to Brawn GP.

Then, in a remarkable run from 2010 to 2013, Red Bull Racing and its drivers won all the drivers' titles and all the constructors' titles. This streak of success propelled the team to sixth in the chart for all-time wins and for fastest laps and up to fifth in the number of pole positions, making up considerable ground on teams that have been around for decades longer. In 2013 alone, there were 19 rounds, of which Red Bull Racing won 13, thanks to Vettel who waltzed clear to claim his fourth title in a row.

Last year wasn't so easy as the teams adapted to the new turbocharged 1.6-litre engine formula. The Renault V6 was no match for the Mercedes counterpart in particular, losing out both in terms of top end horsepower and also in terms of reliability. Former Caterham team chief Cyril Abiteboul was recruited by Renault to put things right. Newey's RB10 chassis seemed to be a good one, but even if Renault achieves its pledge of making strides to re-establish cutting edge performance, drivers Daniel Ricciardo and Daniil Kvyat know that this year's RB11 will be the last F1 product of Newey's fertile mind as he plans to move on to other design interests under the Red Bull New Technologies banner, allegedly including a boat for America's Cup yachting.

One interesting element of the season ahead is that Ricciardo stepped up from Red Bull's junior team last year, Scuderia Toro Rosso, and outperformed Vettel in their first year together. For 2015, Kvyat has followed in the Australian's footsteps and moved up from Scuderia Toro Rosso to replace Vettel who has headed to Ferrari.

> "The engine's reliability was unacceptable and the performance was unacceptable. There needed to be change at Renault, as it couldn't continue like that."
> **Christian Horner**

Ricciardo is now undisputed leader, but it will be intriguing to see how hard he'll be pushed.

DANIEL RICCIARDO

People said that he'd be crushed by Sebastian Vettel when he moved to
Red Bull Racing in 2014. Not only was this quite wrong, but Daniel became
a grand prix winner and a de facto team leader plus a likely future champion.

Daniel was no different to any of his rivals in that he started racing karts as soon as he was old enough. This was in 2000, when he was 10. Living in Western Australia meant that he had to stay close to home, as the costs of crossing Australia to race in the assorted national championships was prohibitive.

Stepping up to Formula Ford in 2005 when he turned 16, Daniel showed enough speed to merit promotion to Asian Formula BMW, a series for which most of the rounds were about as close to his family home in Perth as the east coast of Australia. After ranking third, he moved to Italian Formula Renault in 2007 and did well enough to land Red Bull backing for 2008. He finished the year as runner-up to Valtteri Bottas in the prestigious European series.

Contesting the British F3 Championship has long been seen as a yardstick – former champions include Ayrton Senna and Mika Hakkinen – so Daniel was delighted to add his name to that roll of honour in 2009.

Moving up to more powerful Formula Renault 3.5 in 2010, he lost out to Mikhail Aleshin at the final round. Staying on for 2011, Daniel missed the first two rounds but

Daniel smiles a great deal, but will he
have even more to smile about in 2015?

then got back into the groove, winning at Monza and Monaco. His focus then moved to F1 after tail-end HRT brought him in to replace Narain Karthikeyan midway through the season. Having already tested in F1 for Scuderia Toro Rosso, he wasn't overawed

and did well enough to be promoted to Toro Rosso's race line-up for 2012. Four ninth-place finishes and two 10ths were his tally.

The pressure increased in 2013 when it became clear that Mark Webber might be leaving Red Bull Racing, thus presenting the most enticing opening in F1 in decades, and Daniel won the tussle with team-mate Jean-Eric Vergne for promotion in 2014 after twice finishing seventh.

For all of the flashes of promise, not one F1 expert was able to predict what would follow in 2014, as Daniel mastered the technique required for driving the new-generation cars.

TRACK NOTES

Nationality:	AUSTRALIAN
Born:	1 JULY 1989, PERTH, AUSTRALIA
Website:	www.danielricciardo.com
Teams:	HRT 2011, TORO ROSSO 2012-13, RED BULL RACING 2014-15

CAREER RECORD	
First Grand Prix:	2011 BRITISH GP
Grand Prix starts:	69
Grand Prix wins:	3
2014 Canadian GP, Hungarian GP, Belgian GP	
Poles:	0
Fastest laps:	1
Points:	268
Honours:	2010 FORMULA RENAULT 3.5 RUNNER-UP, 2009 BRITISH FORMULA THREE CHAMPION, 2008 EUROPEAN FORMULA RENAULT RUNNER-UP & WESTERN EUROPEAN FORMULA RENAULT CHAMPION

GETTING THE BETTER OF VETTEL

The move from Scuderia Toro Rosso to Red Bull Racing in place of Mark Webber was always going to be a big step, but ever-smiling Daniel took everything in his stride. Impressively, he not only refused to be cowed by racing alongside a four-time World Champion, but also got to grips with 2014's new type of car better than Vettel did. Daniel bounced back from the disappointment of having second place taken away from him at the opening round in Melbourne for fuel-flow irregularities to start recording strong finishes and then race to a famous win in Canada. Amazingly, it took until the sixth occasion that both drivers finished for Vettel to finish in front. Then, through adding further wins in Hungary and Belgium, Daniel proved the most effective chaser of the dominant Mercedes and is now in place as RBR's crown prince, having proved himself ready to take over as its team leader now that Vettel is moving on. Webber can only applaud his young compatriot's form and fortune.

DANIIL KYVAT

Daniil's maiden season in Formula One was a considerable success as he added experience and maturity to his youthful talent. Now that he is thus armed, it will be interesting to see how much more he can advance in the season ahead.

It's fair to say that Daniil was short on racing experience when he hit F1 last March with Scuderia Toro Rosso. He had been a hit in his brief career in kart racing but, from his graduation from karts to cars, just four seasons elapsed before he was lining up on the grid for last year's Australia GP in Melbourne.

Daniil's first step in cars was in 2010, when he raced for EuroInternational In the European Formula BMW Championship, starting just a couple of weeks after his 16th birthday and peaking with a second place in the final round. He also contested several rounds of the Asian series and scored two wins at Sepang in that.

Wanting to maximize his experience, Daniil then turned his back on a cold winter at home in Russia and contested the Toyota Racing Series in New Zealand, ranking fifth in a series won by Mitch Evans. This set him up for his main 2011 campaign, in Formula Renault in Europe, and he finished third in that as Robin Frijns won the title while being runner-up to his 2015 STR replacement Carlos Sainz Jr in the lesser Northern European championship.

Back for more of the same in 2012, now

Daniil impressed in his rookie year and has been handed an amazing opportunity.

as a fully fledged member of the Red Bull Junior Team, Daniil was pipped by Stoffel Vandoorne in the European championship and won the ALPS region series.

Stepping up to GP3 for 2013, Daniil joined MW Arden and claimed five wins to become champion as he showed marked improvement through the season. For most drivers, this would have been the prelude to a move to GP2 or Formula Renault 3.5, but he was slotted into the F1 seat vacated by Daniel Ricciardo. It was seen by some as a move that had been made a year too soon, but the aplomb with which he adapted to F1 was remarkable. No learning season was needed.

For 2015, of course, Daniil has advanced to the team that dominated from 2010 to 2013. He'll be up against a driver who took the 2014 season by storm - Daniel Ricciardo - and will be out to try to do the same.

TRACK NOTES

Nationality:	RUSSIAN
Born:	26 APRIL 1994, UFA, RUSSIA
Website:	www.daniilkvyat.me
Teams:	TORO ROSSO 2014, RED BULL RACING 2015

CAREER RECORD	
First Grand Prix:	2014 AUSTRALIAN GP
Grand Prix starts:	19
Grand Prix wins:	0
	(best result: 9th, 2014 Australian GP & British GP & Belgian GP)
Poles:	0
Fastest laps:	0
Points:	8
Honours:	2013 GP3 CHAMPION, 2012 FORMULA RENAULT RUNNER-UP & ALPS CHAMPION, 2011 FORMULA RENAULT NORTHERN EUROPE RUNNER-UP, 2009 WSK KART RUNNER-UP

STRAIGHT INTO THE POINTS

Any drive that puts a Toro Rosso into the points is a good one, and so it was a great day for the team at last year's season-opener in Australia as both of the team's drivers scored. Jean-Eric Vergne came home eighth, but his rookie team-mate was just 3s and one place behind, in ninth. Proving that this was no fluke, the still 19-year-old Russian then claimed a couple of 10th place finishes in the next three grands prix, at Sepang and then Shanghai. What really impressed was the way that Daniil seemed calm in this new environment, not fazed by the considerable step up from the GP3 Championship, able simply to focus on the raft of new pressures that F1 brings. When the STR9 proved capable of points, the 20-year-old Russian was generally able to collect. That he was the match for Vergne for pace was impressive indeed. So strong were his race performances too, that Daniil turned out to be one of those rare things, a Red Bull junior who got to achieve their dream, to be promoted to Red Bull Racing.

WILLIAMS

The undoubted feel-good story of 2014 was the return to form of Williams. The once great team will be looking to build on this and has kept both Valtteri Bottas and Felipe Massa to do the job in hand and see whether it can close in on Mercedes.

All fans were delighted by the return of the long-standing Williams to the sharp end of the field in 2014, with Valtteri Bottas leading the way.

It's often said that when Ferrari is strong, F1 is strong. However, some might prefer to substitute Williams for Ferrari because this is a racing team, pure and simple - and F1 tends to be at its best when the teams shine rather than the manufacturers.

When Sir Frank Williams was plain Frank Williams and was making his first forays into F1 in the 1970s, this former racer wasn't tipped to succeed. Far from it: he was short of money and survival seemed to be his only goal, not success. Yet, he kept going and then, after forming Williams Grand Prix Engineering with Patrick Head in 1977 and landing backing, he moved up a gear.

With Alan Jones in the cockpit and Head building the best ground-effects chassis of 1979, the team started winning, first with Clay Regazzoni and then with Jones. The wins kept coming in 1980 and Jones became the team's first world champion as he and Carlos Reutemann guided Williams to its first constructors' title. A second title followed in 1981, but Reutemann fell at the last

to be runner-up to Brabham's Nelson Piquet.

The second purple patch for Williams came in the mid-1980s, when Nigel Mansell led the team's attack. He too fell at the final

round, losing the title to McLaren's Alain Prost when his FW11 had a blow-out. Piquet then went one better in 1987 as Williams took its fourth constructors' crown.

THE POWER AND THE GLORY

PAT SYMONDS
Much of the credit for Williams' turnaround can be laid at this man's feet. A Formula Ford designer in the 1970s, he hit F1 with Toleman in 1982. Pat remained with the team as it metamorphosed into Benetton and worked with Michael Schumacher in his first championship-clinching year. Staying on as engineering chief while it changed name again, to Renault, Pat was asked to leave F1 because of his role in "Singaporegate", but returned as an advisor for Marussia in 2013 and joined Williams last year.

RE-ESTABLISHING THIS ONCE GREAT TEAM
The team's change from Renault engines to Mercedes for last year was one of the key factors to Williams' upswing in fortune, as it was the pick of the bunch. Yet, there was much more to the team challenging for wins, making itself sometimes the best of the rest behind Mercedes GP. Undoubtedly, Felipe Massa and especially Valtteri Bottas did their bit, but the FW36 chassis was a good one. Sometimes too conservative of tactic, the team is getting used to life at the front again.

2014 DRIVERS & RESULTS

Driver	Nationality	Races	Wins	Pts	Pos
Felipe Massa	Brazilian	19	0	134	7th
Valtteri Bottas	Finnish	19	0	186	4th

FOR THE RECORD

Country of origin:	England
Team base:	Grove, England
Telephone:	(44) 01235 777700
Website:	www.williamsf1.com
Active in Formula One:	From 1972
Grands Prix contested:	681
Wins:	114
Pole positions:	128
Fastest laps:	133

THE TEAM

Team principal:	Sir Frank Williams
Co-founder:	Patrick Head
Deputy team principal:	Claire Williams
Chief executive officer:	Mike O'Driscoll
Chief technical officer:	Pat Symonds
Chief designer:	Ed Wood
Head of aerodynamics:	Jason Somerville
Head of aero performance:	Dave Wheater
Head of vehicle dynamics:	Craig Wilson
Head of performance engineering:	Rob Smedley
Head of eng operations:	Jakob Andreasen
Sporting manager:	Steve Nielsen
Test driver:	Susie Wolff
Chassis:	Williams FW37
Engine:	Mercedes V6
Tyres:	Pirelli

By 1992, now with Renault power, Williams was back at the top again, its FW14B the class of the field as Mansell powered to the title. The following year was Prost's turn. Williams looked set to make it a hat trick in 1994, but Michael Schumacher's swerve into Damon Hill at the Adelaide finale stopped that. His combined efforts with David Coulthard's were good enough for the team's seventh constructors' title, though. This would prove a difficult year for Williams, however: it had finally achieved its dream of signing Ayrton Senna, only for him to be killed in the third round at Imola. Bouncing back from that tested the team's mettle. Nor was this the first time that it had had to do so: Frank had been involved in a car crash returning from a pre-season test in 1986 and broke his neck, and he has been in a wheelchair ever since.

In 1996, Williams was back on top and Hill beat Schumacher to the title. In 1997, another second-generation racer, Jacques Villeneuve, took over as team leader and matched his feat.

It seemed unlikely at this point that Williams would ever be anywhere other than at the front, but the rise of McLaren in 1998 moved Williams down the order, and Schumacher's five-year run for Ferrari then pushed it further into the shadows.

From 2000 to 2005 the team was in partnership with BMW, and Ralf Schumacher and Juan Pablo Montoya were both winning races, pushing Ferrari notably hard in 2003. This spell of success came to an end, and the once mighty Williams found itself without a works engine deal for the first time in decades, having to race with customer Cosworth units. Unsurprisingly, results went downhill regardless of what this team of racers tried.

A return to Renault power in 2012 didn't look to be working well, but then Pastor Maldonado won in Spain. This was never repeated and it took a change to Mercedes power in 2014, and the talents of its former test driver Valtteri Bottas and Felipe Massa, to put the team back at the sharp end.

"Felipe is a pleasure to work with and combines raw pace with a wealth of experience, while we have known for many years that Valtteri is a very special talent."
Sir Frank Williams

Team founders Sir Frank Williams and Patrick Head together in the team's early days in 1980.

This popular Brazilian found that there can be life after Ferrari, being reinvigorated at Williams. However, he was bettered by his young team-mate Valtteri Bottas, which will have taken the edge off that. How he responds in 2015 will be intriguing.

There has long been a recognized route to F1, albeit one that changes as new formulae come and go and the ladder is reorganized. However, at the time of his approach in 2001, Felipe was most definitely not racing where the F1 talent-spotters would have been looking. Had he been in the FIA International Formula 3000 Championship, he would have been noticed. Instead, after winning the Brazilian Formula Chevrolet Championship in 1999 and the European and Italian Formula Renault titles in 2000, he contested the second division Euro F3000 series. The cars were little slower than the FIA series cars, but the drivers were. Instead of racing against Mark Webber, Justin Wilson and Antonio Pizzonia, he was up against a group of drivers who have since gone little further. Yet he dominated and did enough to convince Sauber to give him an F1 test. The Swiss team saw a spark of talent and this was his big break.

Racing for Sauber in 2002, he was fast but wild. Managed by Nicolas Todt, son of Ferrari team chief Jean Todt, Felipe then spent a year as Ferrari's test driver. This calmed him down and he matured over the next two years with Sauber. Then

Massa settled in well last year, and came on strong to challenge team-mate Bottas.

Ferrari drew him in to its race team to be team-mate to Michael Schumacher, and he started eight years with them. This brought his first F1 win at the 2006 Turkish GP and the world title for a few fleeting moments in 2008 before he was usurped by Lewis Hamilton at the end of the final lap.

Unfortunately, Felipe also suffered a serious head injury when he was hit on the helmet by an errant spring at the Hungaroring in 2009.

Recovery from that head injury has been gradual, but the signs are that flashes of his raw speed are returning. Late last year, Felipe came back to something like his best form and was able increasingly to keep his highly ranked Williams team-mate Valtteri Bottas on his toes.

TRACK NOTES

Nationality:	BRAZILIAN
Born:	25 APRIL 1981, SAO PAULO, BRAZIL
Website:	www.felipemassa.com
Teams:	SAUBER 2002 & 2004-05,
	FERRARI 2006-13, WILLIAMS 2014-15

CAREER RECORD

First Grand Prix:	2002 AUSTRALIAN GP
Grand Prix starts:	211
Grand Prix wins:	11
2006 Turkish GP, Brazilian GP, 2007 Bahrain GP, Spanish GP, Turkish GP, 2008 Bahrain GP, Turkish GP, French GP, European GP, Belgian GP, Brazilian GP	
Poles:	16
Fastest laps:	6
Points:	950
Honours:	2008 FORMULA ONE RUNNER-UP, 2001 EUROPEAN FORMULA 3000 CHAMPION, 2000 EUROPEAN & ITALIAN FORMULA RENAULT CHAMPION, 1999 BRAZILIAN FORMULA CHEVROLET CHAMPION

A RETURN TO THE PODIUM

One had to feel for Felipe in his last few campaigns with Ferrari, where he was able to take only a supporting role, racing almost in a different sphere to clear team number one Fernando Alonso. Moving to Williams for 2014 clearly reinvigorated him because it removed those pressures. Better than that, his Williams FW36 was frequently more competitive than the Ferrari F14 T. So, apart from being taken out at the first corner of the season-opening race in Melbourne, life was good. As the season progressed, there was clearly nothing that he could do about the dominant pace of the Mercedes duo, but racing for a team on the upswing ensured that the atmosphere at Williams was fantastic. Pole position for the Austrian GP at the Red Bull Ring was a thrill, but the downside was that inexperienced team-mate Valtteri Bottas was collecting podium appearances by the handful. Fortunately, Felipe made the podium by finishing in third place at Monza and peaked with second at the final round.

⊕ VALTTERI BOTTAS

No driver made more of an impression in 2014 than this quietly determined Finn, who combined his second year of racing in F1 with an increasingly competitive Williams. He drove the car with appreciable craft and guile as well as speed.

Valtteri raced karts with success on the Scandinavian scene, hoping no doubt to emulate the success of compatriot Mika Hakkinen, who landed two F1 titles with McLaren when Valtteri was still a schoolboy in Nastola.

Stepping up to car racing as soon as he was old enough, Valtteri competed in Formula Renault in 2007, finishing third in the Northern European series. In 2008, he won the Northern European title and edged out Daniel Ricciardo for the more prestigious European title for the Motopark Academy team.

Formula 3 was the next step and Valtteri made his mark in that, ending the year third in a European Championship that was won comfortably by his ART Grand Prix team-mate Jules Bianchi ahead of Christian Vietoris. Finishing second six times, Valtteri managed to come out on top in the Masters F3 race at Zandvoort. Returning to take a shot at the title in 2010, Valtteri won twice but again ranked third, with Edoardo Mortara being crowned champion. Again he took victory in the Masters race.

So, for 2011, knowing that he needed to land a title to progress, Valtteri tried

Valtteri turned definite talent in 2014 and is highly tipped to go on to greater things.

the GP3 series and succeeded. This gave him the boost he needed, although he was already on Williams's books and had secured his first F1 test runs.

Without the backing to take a shot at Formula Renault 3.5 or GP2 (the traditional

last staging posts before F1), Valtteri immersed himself in Williams and was given the opportunity of running in first practice sessions on grand prix Fridays, not only gaining valuable track time but also showing the team what he could do.

Suitably impressed, Williams gave him a race seat for 2013 and Valtteri qualified a surprise third in the wet for the Canadian GP in Montreal, then finishing eighth in the US GP when the car was more competitive. Valtteri ended the year with more points than his vastly more experienced team-mate Pastor Maldonado, and the team was more than happy to keep this straightforward and unflappable racer on its books for 2014. Its decision to do so was the right one, judging by his 2014 form.

THE STAR OF THE SEASON

The Williams team had always spoken of great things when describing Valtteri's performances when he was serving first as its test driver in 2011 and then as its reserve driver in 2012. The team knew that its FW35 was no great car in 2013. Yet, what the Finn achieved in 2014 was probably beyond even their predictions. He was a driver who belied his lack of F1 racing experience to produce drives from the very top drawer. Armed with a competitive car for the first time, he was one of the stars of the season-opener in Melbourne and would probably have reached the podium had he not clipped a wall. He landed his first top-three result at the Austrian GP and then proved that this was no flash in the pan, adding three more podiums in the next four races. Had the Mercedes GP duo not been so dominant, his second year with Williams might have landed a victory. That more than a few paddock insiders describe him as a future champion says it all.

TRACK NOTES

Nationality:	FINNISH
Born:	28 AUGUST 1989, TOWN, FINLAND
Website:	www.valtteribottas.com
Teams:	WILLIAMS 2013-2015

CAREER RECORD

First Grand Prix:	2013 AUSTRALIAN GP
Grand Prix starts:	38
Grand Prix wins:	0
(best result: 2nd, 2014 British & German GPs)	
Poles:	0
Fastest laps:	1
Points:	190
Honours:	2011 GP3 CHAMPION, 2010 & 2009 MASTERS FORMULA 3 WINNER, 2008 EUROPEAN & NORTHERN EUROPEAN FORMULA RENAULT CHAMPION

Nico Rosberg leads McLaren's Jenson Button and Kevin Magnussen and Mercedes team-mate Lewis Hamilton into Luffield on the opening lap of last year's British GP.

SCUDERIA FERRARI

This is a team that was founded in 1946, took part in F1's first World Championship (1950), and is the world's most famous team. After a poor 2014, though, it needs to hit form again, with many personnel changes made in the hope of achieving this.

Ferrari will be without Fernando Alonso's driving force this year and will need to earn its stripes again if it's to return to winning.

Enzo Ferrari was a racing driver who turned to team management. He was asked to run Alfa Romeo's works team in the 1930s, but the relationship was not to last, and he ran a car bearing his surname for the first time in 1946. Ferrari's first win of note came in the 1949 Swiss GP and the red livery with a badge denoting a black prancing horse on a yellow background has been its colour scheme ever since.

Ferrari wasn't present at the inaugural round of the World Championship in 1950, but was there for the second, at Monaco, where Alberto Ascari finished second. Alfa Romeo dominated the year, but then withdrew and so Ferrari began winning in 1951, with Jose Froilan Gonzalez taking its first, at Silverstone. A change of rules made the World Championship run to F2 regulations in 1952 and 1953, and Ascari won both titles. After a brief period of Mercedes domination, Juan Manuel Fangio won the 1956 title in a Ferrari-entered Lancia. Two years later, Mike Hawthorn beat Vanwall's

best to come out on top. Then, after another change of F1 regulations, Ferrari was well placed for the 1.5-litre regulations for 1961, and Phil Hill lifted the crown.

By now, there were also constructors' titles up for grabs, which Ferrari won in 1961 and then in 1964 when John Surtees nipped in at the last. After this, though, the

THE POWER AND THE GLORY

JAMES ALLISON
Ferrari's technical director graduated in engineering from Cambridge University. Having specialized in aerodynamics, he found a job in F1 with Benetton. That was in 1991 and he then learned his craft, moving to Larrousse and then returning to Benetton in 1995 after the French team folded. After a short spell with Ferrari, James went back to Benetton after it had been renamed Renault, becoming technical director. In 2012, he moved to take the same role at Ferrari and leads its technical side after its rejig for 2015.

A SEASON OF INTENSE DISAPPOINTMENT
There had been much rejigging of key personnel and the arrival of new F1 regulations did little to help the team advance, especially when its turbo engine was no match for either the Mercedes or Renault V6s. Kimi Raikkonen struggled with the car, and Fernando Alonso propelled it as far up the grid as he was able, but the fact that he was soon linked to other teams for 2015 tells its own story. Some say that the return of former technical chief Ross Brawn is needed.

2014 DRIVERS & RESULTS

Driver	Nationality	Races	Wins	Pts	Pos
Fernando Alonso	Spanish	19	0	161	6th
Kimi Raikkonen	Finnish	19	0	55	12th

FOR THE RECORD

Country of origin:	Italy
Team base:	Maranello, Italy
Telephone:	(39) 536 949111
Website:	www.ferrari.com
Active in Formula One:	From 1950
Grands Prix contested:	870
Wins:	219
Pole positions:	207
Fastest laps:	226

THE TEAM

President:	Sergio Marchionne
Team principal:	Maurizio Arrivabene
Technical director:	James Allison
Chief designer:	Simone Resta
Power unit director:	Mattia Binotto
Chief designer, power unit:	Lorenzo Sassi
Chief aerodynamicist:	Loic Bigois
Sporting director:	Massimo Rivola
Production director:	Corrado Lanzone
Reserve driver:	Esteban Gutierrez
Chassis:	Ferrari F15 T
Engine:	Ferrari V6
Tyres:	Pirelli

British teams took control of F1, powered by innovation, much to Enzo's disgust. It took Niki Lauda to galvanize the team, with Luca de Montezemolo shaking up the management side, before the titles flowed again. Lauder won in 1975 and 1977, and Jody Scheckter was champion for Ferrari in 1979. After that, the team's inability to master ground effects cost it dearly and only once it had done so did it claim titles again, in 1982 and 1983. As far as drivers' titles, though, the cupboard remained bare right through until 2000, when Michael Schumacher ended the drought in his fifth year with the team.

Helped often by the F1 rules being framed according to its strengths and its wishes, Ferrari now took control of F1, led by team chief Jean Todt. Schumacher made the most of the situation to win five titles on the trot. McLaren got back on song in 2007, but Ferrari came good at the last for Kimi Raikkonen to become its next champion. Then, in 2008, it looked as though Felipe Massa had also come from behind to deprive Lewis Hamilton the title, but the Ferrari driver was to be disappointed when the McLaren racer claimed the place that he needed on the final lap to lift the crown.

Yet, the sheer longevity of Ferrari's spell in F1, the longest of any team by far, combined with its spells of excellence leaves it atop the tables for most starts, most wins, most poles, fastest laps and most points, as well as most titles.

Recently it hasn't been able to beat Brawn GP, Red Bull Racing and, in 2014, Mercedes, even with the best efforts of Alonso. Last September, after another year of being less than the best and a period of rumours, di Montezemolo stepped down as Ferrari's chairman after 23 years in the role.

> "I had been to Maranello as a child, trying to look over the fence, so to officially be part of this team feels fantastic. It feels different with everybody wearing red and and everything being red, but it's really something special."
> **Sebastian Vettel**

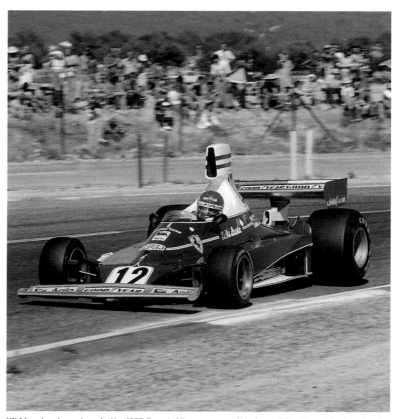

Niki Lauda, shown here in the 1975 French GP, was responsible for putting Ferrari back on track.

Not only did Sebastian's four-year run of F1 titles come to an end last year, but he ended the year as the second-ranked driver in his own team, put in the shadow by Daniel Ricciardo. His response in 2015 after moving to Ferrari will be revealing.

Sebastian has bounded through his career since hitting the car-racing scene in 2003 armed with European junior karting titles. A learning year in Germany's Formula BMW ADAC series was followed by near total domination, winning 18 of the 20 races.

Boosted by Red Bull support, Sebastian advanced to F3 in 2005 and was top rookie as Lewis Hamilton lifted the European crown. At the second time of asking, Sebastian was runner-up to Paul di Resta. However, he emphasized his promise by contesting three rounds of the more powerful Renault World Series and winning two of those. Returning in 2007, Sebastian had started winning again when his F1 break arrived after Robert Kubica was hurt in the Canadian GP. So, a few weeks short of his 20th birthday, he made his debut for BMW Sauber in the US GP, scoring the point for eighth place. Four races later, he was back, with Scuderia Toro Rosso, taking Scott Speed's ride and proving his worth with fourth place in the Chinese GP.

After claiming a maiden win for himself and the team at Monza in 2008, Sebastian was clearly ready for promotion to Red Bull Racing. Runner-up to Jenson Button in 2009, despite scoring four wins, Sebastian

It's all change for Vettel after six years with Red Bull. Will he make himself lead driver?

then overhauled both team-mate Mark Webber and Ferrari's Fernando Alonso to win the 2010 F1 crown to become the youngest ever World Champion.

Three more titles were claimed in the next three years, including 13 wins in 2013,

as Sebastian Vettel took his career tally on to 39 wins.

After his patchy 2014 campaign, Seb's move to Ferrari might do him some good.

TRACK NOTES

Nationality:	GERMAN
Born:	3 JULY 1987, HEPPENHEIM, GERMANY
Website:	www.sebastianvettel.de
Teams:	BMW SAUBER 2007, TORO ROSSO 2007-08, RED BULL RACING 2009-14, FERRARI 2015

CAREER RECORD

First Grand Prix:	2007 UNITED STATES GP
Grand Prix starts:	139
Grand Prix wins:	39

2008 Italian GP, 2009 Chinese GP, British GP, Japanese GP, Abu Dhabi GP, 2010 Malaysian GP, European GP, Japanese GP, Brazilian GP, Abu Dhabi GP, 2011 Australian GP, Malaysian GP, Turkish GP, Spanish GP, Monaco GP, European GP, Belgian GP, Italian GP, Singapore GP, Korean GP, Indian GP, 2012 Bahrain GP, Singapore GP, Japanese GP, Korean GP, Indian GP, 2013 Malaysian GP, Bahrain GP, Canadian GP, German GP, Belgian GP, Italian GP, Singapore GP, Korean GP, Japanese GP, Indian GP, Abu Dhabi GP, United States GP, Brazilian GP

Poles:	45
Fastest laps:	24
Points:	1618
Honours:	2010, 2011, 2012 & 2013 FORMULA ONE WORLD CHAMPION, 2009 FORMULA ONE RUNNER-UP, 2006 EUROPEAN FORMULA THREE RUNNER-UP, 2004 GERMAN FORMULA BMW ADAC CHAMPION, 2003 GERMAN FORMULA BMW ADAC RUNNER-UP, 2001 EUROPEAN & GERMAN JUNIOR KART CHAMPION

RACING A CAR HE DIDN'T LIKE

Being outqualified by team-mate Daniel Ricciardo at the opening round was permissible because the weather had turned the event into a lottery, but as the season continued it became clear that the young Australian had the upper hand. Put simply, Sebastian was struggling to get the feel he required from the Red Bull RB10. Unable to set it up as he liked, he found himself wearing his tyres more. There were times that Sebastian seemed less than focused, dropping from the famously high levels of concentration that had won him those four titles. At other times, such as his drive from 15th to fourth in the Spanish GP, he was back to his best. Later in the year, as the RB10 picked up its pace, Sebastian was able to see the light, taking second place behind Lewis Hamilton in Singapore to show that he was still in the hunt. He will have learned many important lessons about himself during a year in which his team's car was not the pick of the pack.

Last year was not Kimi's finest. Brought back to Ferrari to rack up the points, he didn't like the car and underperformed. Whether he has the motivation to do better in 2015, when he'll have Sebastian Vettel as team-mate, remains to be seen.

Not someone to do things by the book, Kimi set a record for brevity when he advanced from karts to F1 after just 23 cars races. More than that, by not racing in either F3 and then something more powerful like GP2, he effectively jumped two steps of the ladder. Such was his sangfroid, he never looked anything other than ready when he joined Sauber as a 21-year-old in 2001.

Kimi had been the star of the Finnish and Scandinavian karting scene in the late 1990s and been European championship runner-up. It was at this point that he was spotted by the Robertsons, with former racer Steve becoming his manager.

This was fortuitous, as their boldness resulted in Kimi landing an F1 test with Sauber. Peter Sauber didn't need a second look and Kimi was contracted for 2001. Amazingly, he finished sixth on his debut and, before long, McLaren had his name on a contract for the following year. Runner-up to Ferrari's Michael Schumacher in 2003, falling just two points short, he was second again in 2005, to Renault's Fernando Alonso. Then, in 2007, now with Ferrari, he stole the title from McLaren's Alonso and Lewis Hamilton by winning the final round.

Kimi will be hoping he can get to grips with this year's Ferrari to rediscover his spark.

Then, after ranking only sixth in 2009 and having become truly fed up with the promotional demands all drivers are expected to face as part of their role, Kimi was happy to be bought out of his Ferrari contract and went rallying with Citroen

instead, in the World Championship no less. Fast but prone to accidents, Kimi then returned to F1 with Lotus in 2012 and won the Abu Dhabi GP, then adding another win at Melbourne in the 2013 opener before joining Ferrari for a second spell.

TRACK NOTES

Nationality:	FINNISH
Born:	17 OCTOBER 1979, ESPOO, FINLAND
Website:	www.kimiraikkonen.com
Teams:	SAUBER 2001, McLAREN 2002-06, FERRARI 2007-09, LOTUS 2012-13, FERRARI 2014-15

CAREER RECORD

First Grand Prix:	2001 AUSTRALIAN GP
Grand Prix starts:	213
Grand Prix wins:	20
	2003 Malaysian GP, 2004 Belgian GP, 2005 Spanish GP, Monaco GP, Canadian GP, Hungarian GP, Turkish GP, Belgian GP, Japanese GP, 2007 Australian GP, French GP, British GP, Belgian GP, Chinese GP, Brazilian GP, 2008 Malaysian GP, Spanish GP, 2009 Belgian GP, 2012 Abu Dhabi GP, 2013 Australian GP
Poles:	16
Fastest laps:	40
Points:	1024
Honours:	2007 FORMULA ONE WORLD CHAMPION, 2003 & 2005 FORMULA ONE RUNNER-UP, 2000 BRITISH FORMULA RENAULT CHAMPION, 1999 BRITISH FORMULA RENAULT WINTER SERIES CHAMPION, 1998 EUROPEAN SUPER A KART RUNNER-UP, FINNISH KART CHAMPION & NORDIC KART CHAMPION

FINDING HIS CAR HARD TO DRIVE

The long and the short of Kimi's return to Ferrari in 2014 was that he found the car very difficult to get to grips with. Furthermore, its new V6 turbo engine was clearly no match for the rival Mercedes unit. So, combining these two factors might explain some of his inability to gather points race by race as he always has in the past. That team-mate Fernando Alonso was almost invariably way ahead in both qualifying and the races, even stepping onto the podium from time to time, made his efforts look all the less impressive. Some said that his motivation was gone too. Losing a good result in Monaco when he was hit by Max Chilton during a safety car period was unlucky, but Kimi got it together and scored a good fourth place at Spa-Francorchamps. Yet, with Alonso looking to quit the team, his place is safe for this year at least, dispelling talk that surfaced midway through last year to suggest that he might not see out his two-year contract.

Balcony space is at a premium for the Monaco GP, with these lucky fans looking down on the ascent to Massenet. The 2014 race ended with one-two for Mercedes (Rosberg–Hamilton) and a third-place podium finish for Daniel Ricciardo.

McLAREN

Two uncompetitive seasons in a row for a team as established and well-funded as McLaren is simply not good enough, and Ron Dennis has made wholesale changes to make it competitive again. Former hunting partner Honda has now joined the party.

Kevin Magnussen discovered last December that it would be he, not Jenson Button, who would stand down to make way for Fernando Alonso.

This will be McLaren's 50th year in the World Championship and it remains one of the most successful teams of all, albeit one in need of an upswing of form. Across the 49 years to date, it has won 12 drivers' championship titles and eight times ended the year atop the constructors' table. What it craves as it welcomes Honda back as its engine supplier for the first time since 1992 is a return to the heady days when its star drivers Ayrton Senna and Alain Prost swept all before them at the end of the 1980s.

The team was founded by Bruce McLaren. The Kiwi was a grand prix winner at the age of only 22 when he triumphed for the works Cooper team at Sebring in 1959. As good an engineer as he was a racing driver, Bruce decided to build his own brand of cars, starting with the M1A sports racer in 1964. It was so good, and its successors better still, that this was soon a lucrative business and the first McLaren F1 car hit the grid at Monaco two years later. The key to McLaren's advancement was two-fold. One

was the financial benefits pouring in as its sportscars dominated the lucrative CanAm sportscar series in North America. The other was the arrival of the Ford Cosworth

DFV, which in 1968 gave him the competitive engine that he'd lacked in McLaren's early F1 forays. The wins started flowing from the fourth round in 1968, when Bruce won

THE POWER AND THE GLORY

RON DENNIS
This is the man who took over McLaren in 1980 and turned it from a midfield team back into a front-running outfit. Ron was a mechanic with Cooper in the 1960s, but his drive for detail and technical excellence was what took McLaren to titles for Lauda, Prost, Hakkinen and Hamilton. He handed over to Martin Whitmarsh in 2009 to focus on McLaren's road cars. Last year, Ron returned, with Whitmarsh being moved aside to give the team a hard edge again.

FAILING TO GET THE FRONT END RIGHT
This wasn't a great year for McLaren after a torrid time in testing. Despite using superior Mercedes engines, the team struggled. Second and third in the opening race for rookie Kevin Magnussen and Jenson Button suggested a great season ahead, but those results flattered the performance of the MP4-29s and neither would visit the podium again. With Honda engines arriving for 2015, the Abu Dhabi GP brought an end to the team's 20-year association with Mercedes and the team can only hope for greater things on all fronts.

2014 DRIVERS & RESULTS

Driver	Nationality	Races	Wins	Pts	Pos
Jenson Button	British	19	0	126	8th
Kevin Magnussen	Danish	19	0	55	11th

FOR THE RECORD

Country of origin:	England
Team base:	Woking, England
Telephone:	(44) 01483 261000
Website:	www.mclaren.com
Active in Formula One:	From 1966
Grands Prix contested:	762
Wins:	181
Pole positions:	154
Fastest laps:	152

THE TEAM

Chairman:	Ron Dennis
Racing director:	Eric Boullier
Managing director:	Jonathan Neale
Technical director:	Tim Goss
Engineering director:	Matt Morris
Chief engineer:	Peter Prodromou
Director of design & development	Neil Oatley
Head of aerodynamics:	tba
Operations director:	Simon Roberts
Sporting director:	tba
Team manager:	David Redding
Principal race engineer:	Ciaron Pilbeam
Chief mechanic:	Jonathan Brookes
Test driver:	Kevin Magnussen
Chassis:	McLaren MP4-30
Engine:	Honda V6
Tyres:	Pirelli

in Belgium, and his fellow New Zealander Denny Hulme soon took over as the team's sharpest tool. The team was rocked in 1970, however, when Bruce was killed testing at Goodwood, but team manager Teddy Mayer steadied the ship.

The first driver to turn McLaren into a title-winning team was Emerson Fittipaldi in 1974. A champion two years earlier for Lotus, he won three times to pip Ferrari's Clay Regazzoni, with supporting drives from Hulme helping McLaren to its first constructors' title. The M23 was still competitive two years later when James Hunt was McLaren's next champion. However, McLaren was slow to harness ground effects and slipped down the order as Williams came to the fore. Indeed, the lack of form led to a change of management, with Ron Dennis arriving to first work with and then take over from Mayer. The fruits of his organization were clear by 1984, when Niki Lauda became McLaren's third champion. He did so by just half a point from team-mate Alain Prost and the Frenchman then won the title in 1985 and again in 1986, stealing it at the last from Nigel Mansell.

Prost would win the title for a third time in 1989, by which time he was paired with Ayrton Senna, who had joined him the year earlier to win the title at his first attempt, the team dominating thanks to Honda turbo power. The two men were so far clear of their rivals that the battle became a personal one, too personal at times, and Prost elected to join Ferrari for 1990. Even so, he couldn't prevent Senna from claiming his second crown, and a third in 1991.

After Honda pulled out at the end of 1992, McLaren struggled to find a good engine partner until Mercedes joined the show, with Adrian Newey penning title-winning cars for Mika Hakkinen in 1998 and 1999. Most recently, Lewis Hamilton landed the drivers' title in 2008, making up for when he and Fernando Alonso were pipped by Ferrari's Kimi Raikkonen at the final round in 2007.

Helping it to stand above most teams, McLaren has a lucrative supercar division that enables it to fill its coffers.

"McLaren is a top team, a big team with a lot of history, and we want to be back where we should be. We are still pushing and will take the time we need."
Eric Boullier

McLaren was never greater than when Senna and Prost were fighting each other for glory in 1988.

It was widely discussed last year that Fernando might move on from Ferrari, angered by its poor form. Then he did, to McLaren. What remains clear is that he's a driver with another world championship title within him. He just needs the tools for the job.

Nobody can deny that Fernando is one of the very best drivers in F1. Not just now, but ever. He has been a star in every category that he has contested, both kart and car, and he has been limited to just two world titles simply by not having been in the very best team during most of his F1 career.

The star of the Spanish karting scene, he stepped up to become World Kart Champion in 1996. As he had to wait until he was 18 to start racing cars, he added a further Spanish karting title and an Italian one too before graduating to car racing in 1999.

This took the form of Formula Nissan – and he walked the championship. His second year in cars was in F3000, just one step below F1, and he impressed from his first race. His win at Spa-Francorchamps was a dominant performance that is still talked about.

Fernando was clearly ready for F1 and got his break with Minardi in 2001. With Flavio Briatore taking him under his wing, Fernando spent 2002 as Renault test driver, then raced for the team for the next four years. He became a grand prix winner in 2003 and then World Champion in both 2005 and 2006.

Fernando is determined that his second spell at McLaren will be more fruitful than his first.

His move to McLaren ought to have given him a third title, but Fernando and the team fell out, so he returned to a now less competitive Renault. Ferrari then needed a new team leader after Kimi Raikkonen's departure and Fernando went there in 2010.

Frustration in the final race, at Abu Dhabi, denied Fernando his third F1 crown, with Sebastian Vettel coming through to take the honours. He was runner-up to Vettel again in 2012 and became increasingly desperate to give himself a winning chance again.

TRACK NOTES

Nationality:	SPANISH
Born:	29 JULY 1981, OVIEDO, SPAIN
Website:	www.fernandoalonso.com
Teams:	MINARDI 2001, RENAULT 2003-06, McLAREN 2007, RENAULT 2008-09, FERRARI 2010-14, McLAREN 2015

CAREER RECORD

First Grand Prix:	2001 AUSTRALIAN GP
Grand Prix starts:	236
Grand Prix wins:	32

2003 Hungarian GP, 2005 Malaysian GP, Bahrain GP, San Marino GP, European GP, French GP, German GP, Chinese GP, 2006 Bahrain GP, Australian GP, Spanish GP, Monaco GP, British GP, Canadian GP, Japanese GP, 2007 Malaysian GP, Monaco GP, European GP, Italian GP, 2008 Singapore GP, Japanese GP, 2010 Australian GP, German GP, Italian GP, Singapore GP, Korean GP, 2011 British GP, 2012 Malaysian GP, European GP, German GP, 2013 Chinese GP, Spanish GP

Poles:	22
Fastest laps:	21
Points:	1767

Honours: 2005 & 2006 FORMULA ONE WORLD CHAMPION, 2010, 2012 & 2013 FORMULA ONE RUNNER-UP, 1999 FORMULA NISSAN CHAMPION, 1997 ITALIAN & SPANISH KART CHAMPION, 1996 WORLD & SPANISH KART CHAMPION, 1994 & 1995 SPANISH JUNIOR KART CHAMPION

MAKING THE BEST OF A DONKEY

It's always been acknowledged that Fernando is a driver who will extract the maximum out of a car – not just over a flying lap but over an entire race. In the past, he has taken cars closer to the front of the field than they deserved, and this was no different with last year's Ferrari F14 T. Team-mate Kimi Raikkonen was bamboozled by the car, picking up only the odd point here or there. Fernando, though, was on mighty form: struggling with its lack of top speed, he made a podium visit whenever possible. Twice only – at Shanghai and the Hungaroring – but he showed his mettle by scoring good helpings of points almost every time out. Ironically, this run was broken by retirement from the team's home race at Monza, when he was again bemoaning the F14 T's performance. Much of the year was overshadowed by talk of whether Fernando would quit the team, which was certainly a distraction, but he kept performing exceptionally while plotting his future.

McLaren was far from its best in 2014 and Jenson had a frustrating year as former team-mate Lewis Hamilton starred for Mercedes. For 2015, however, hope comes in the form of new engine partner Honda, as Jenson enters his 16th year of F1.

Jenson won the British cadet title at the age of 11 in 1991. After winning the European Super A title in 1997, he graduated to cars and not only won the British Formula Ford title but the Festival too. Best of all, he landed the McLaren Autosport BRDC Young Driver award and, with it, an F1 test.

Moving up to Formula 3 in 1999, Jenson was immediately on the pace and ranked third as Marc Hynes took the title. Then, at a point when most would be trying to land a ride in F3000, his management landed him an F1 test with Ligier. He shone, and so his career took a different course: he was involved in a shoot-out for the second Williams seat for 2000. Thus, at the 11th hour, he was picked to be the team's number two alongside Ralf Schumacher.

Moving to Benetton for 2001 and staying on when it metamorphosed into Renault delivered little, and in 2003 Jenson joined BAR. He made 10 podium appearances in his second year with them and he ended third overall in a year dominated by Michael Schumacher for Ferrari.

Jenson stayed on and gave the team its reward when it changed its name to Honda Racing for 2006 and he triumphed at the

Jenson held his nerve and kept his drive thanks to strong form late last season.

Hungarian GP. This was a win against the odds in changeable conditions and would be the template for several future wins.

Then, in November 2008, the team closed. But just as his career appeared over, it was given a boost, the team

morphing into Brawn GP and starting 2009 with a clever double-diffuser that produced the fastest car in the field. Six wins later, he was World Champion.

A move to McLaren for 2010 pitted him against Lewis Hamilton and Jenson's best year with the team left him as runner-up in 2011 after taking three wins.

TRACK NOTES

Nationality:	BRITISH
Born:	19 JANUARY 1980, FROME, ENGLAND
Website:	www.jensonbutton.com
Teams:	WILLIAMS 2000, BENETTON/RENAULT 2001-02, BAR/HONDA 2003-08, BRAWN 2009, McLAREN 2010-15

CAREER RECORD

First Grand Prix:	2000 AUSTRALIAN GP
Grand Prix starts:	266
Grand Prix wins:	15
	2006 Hungarian GP, 2009 Australian GP, Malaysian GP, Bahrain GP, Spanish GP, Monaco GP, Turkish GP, 2010 Australian GP, Chinese GP, 2011 Canadian GP, Hungarian GP, Japanese GP, 2012 Australian GP, Belgian GP, Brazilian GP
Poles:	8
Fastest laps:	8
Points:	1198
Honours:	2009 FORMULA ONE WORLD CHAMPION, 1999 MACAU FORMULA THREE RUNNER-UP, 1998 FORMULA FORD FESTIVAL WINNER, BRITISH FORMULA FORD CHAMPION & McLAREN AUTOSPORT BRDC YOUNG DRIVER, 1997 EUROPEAN SUPER A KART CHAMPION, 1991 BRITISH CADET KART CHAMPION

RACING ON WITHOUT JOHN

This was the first year that Jenson went racing without the support of his father John, who died of a heart attack during the winter. An affable character, John provided welcome humour and balance in the paddock, and Jenson had to learn to cope without him. He also had to learn to manage with a McLaren that was almost as far from the pace as its 2013 MP4-28 had been. Take away his third place in the Australian GP, an unusually topsy-turvy season-opener, and there was precious little to shout about through the course of 2014. Even the challenge of rookie team-mate Kevin Magnussen left people wondering whether last season would be Jenson's last year in F1. Yet, his dogged tenacity and application was apparent, especially in finishing fourth in the British GP and then in his run of strong results in four of the final five grands prix, and such expertise is something that Honda will want as it dips its toe back into the F1 pond in the season ahead.

FORCE INDIA

Force India stepped up a gear last year and pushed the more fancied McLaren hard, but the team from Silverstone still has some way to go if it wants to challenge for wins, the last of which it landed in 2003 when the team was entered as Jordan.

Hulkenberg is a driver who delivers whenever the car is good enough, and his battle with Perez is sure to produce plenty more points in 2015.

Racer turned team owner Eddie Jordan advanced from Formula 3 to Formula 3000 and earned plaudits for helping Jean Alesi to the title in 1989. Then, in 1991, he and his team from opposite the main gate at Silverstone made the final step to F1. Their car was simple but effective and rattled the establishment, with Andrea de Cesaris twice finishing fourth. A complication came when driver Bertrand Gachot was jailed for assaulting a London taxi driver. Jordan's solution was to give Michael Schumacher his F1 break as his replacement. Sadly, Benetton coaxed him away before the following race.

Worse was to follow, as Jordan replaced its Ford engines with Yamaha units for 1992 and dropped down the order. It was only after paying for Hart engines in 1993 that the team went forward again, with Rubens Barrichello leading its attack with able support from Eddie Irvine.

Always a popular team for its youthful, slightly anti-establishment image, Jordan hit the big time only when it replaced its Peugeot engines with Mugen Hondas in 1998. Damon Hill was its spearhead, giving the team its first win in the Belgian GP, chased across the line by team-mate Ralf Schumacher to help Jordan rank fourth.

Heinz-Harald Frentzen then joined the team for 1999 and won at both Magny-Cours and Monza to rank third behind McLaren's

THE POWER AND THE GLORY

ANDREW GREEN
Andrew was a designer for leading Formula 3000 chassis manufacturer Reynard before joining the Jordan team as it hit F1 in 1991. After a four-year stint as a designer, he became a race engineer. In 1998, Andrew moved across to Tyrrell as its entry was taken over by British American Racing, and he stayed there in the role of the chief designer until Red Bull Racing signed him in 2005. A spell at Virgin Racing was followed by his return to the team that was once Jordan in 2011 as technical director.

GETTING IN AMONG THE POINTS
Last year was a good one for Force India because the combination of a good chassis and Mercedes' V6 was competitive, enabling Nico Hulkenberg and Sergio Perez to collect points at almost every round. Perez even stood on the podium after finishing third in Bahrain. The Mexican was heading for fourth in Canada before crashing with Felipe Massa at the start of the final lap. Financial concerns continue to hover, but the prize money for ranking sixth will have helped.

2014 DRIVERS & RESULTS

Driver	Nationality	Races	Wins	Pts	Pos
Nico Hulkenberg	German	19	0	96	9th
Sergio Perez	Mexican	18	0	59	10th

FOR THE RECORD

Country of origin:	England
Team base:	Silverstone, England
Telephone:	(44) 01327 850800
Website:	www.forceindiaf1.com
Active in Formula One:	As Jordan
1991-2004, Midland 2005-06, Spyker 2007	
Grands Prix contested:	416
Wins:	4
Pole positions:	3
Fastest laps:	5

THE TEAM

Team principal & managing director:

	Vijay Mallya
Chairman:	Subrata Roy Sahara
Deputy team principal:	Robert Fernley
Chief operating officer:	Otmar Szafnauer
Technical director:	Andrew Green
Production director:	Bob Halliwell
Aerodynamics director:	Simon Phillips
Chief designers:	Akio Haga & Ian Hall
Aerodynamics director:	Simon Phillips
Sporting director:	Andy Stevenson
Test driver:	tba
Chassis:	Force India VJM08
Engine:	Mercedes V6
Tyres:	Pirelli

Mika Hakkinen and Ferrari's Eddie Irvine. The team also finished a distant third in the constructors' rankings, held back by Hill losing his form in the sister car.

Jordan's final win came in 2003 in the third round of the season at Interlagos, when it turned to Ford for its engines again and Giancarlo Fisichella triumphed in a crash-strewn race. This was not repeated, though, and the team's next best result that year was seventh at Indianapolis.

Jordan sold out to Russian steel magnate Alex Shnaider at the end of 2004. He owned it for the next two years, renaming it as Midland for the 2006 season, but it then changed its name again for 2007, when revived Dutch sportscar manufacturer Spyker took the reins. These were not great days for the team: points became a rarity and it seemed clear that the team had to change or die. Enter Indian industrialist and former racer Vijay Mallya, who bought the team and renamed it Force India for 2008. Now racing in a white, orange and green livery, the team looked better than it had for years, though neither Fisichella nor Adrian

Sutil managed to score that year. Things improved marginally in 2009, and in 2010 Sutil was joined by Vitantonio Liuzzi. This was the team's second year with Mercedes power, and it achieved seventh place overall, just one point behind Williams.

Money was always tight, but the team advanced to sixth overall, just a few points behind Renault in 2011 when Sutil was joined by impressive rookie Paul di Resta. It slid back to seventh in 2012, when Nico Hulkenberg gave the team considerable cheer by leading the final round, in Brazil, before crashing into Lewis Hamilton's McLaren. Outperforming Sauber in 2013 enabled Force India to move back to sixth overall, with di Resta peaking with fourth place in Bahrain.

The team then earned a similar ranking last year, but this time was snapping at McLaren's heels in a tussle over fifth place for much of the season, and Sergio Perez gave the team its first podium since its fluky

three-four finish in the largely boycotted 2005 United States GP. Boosted by running Mercedes' class-leading V6 turbo, the team performed for the first time in years in the manner in which it used to as Jordan.

> "From what we can see, Mercedes are going to deliver even more in the future and we just need to do the power unit justice by bolting it to a chassis that has got a bit more performance in it."
>
> **Andrew Green**

Force India started life as Jordan. Here's Damon Hill splashing to its first win, at Spa in 1998.

SERGIO PEREZ

The flashes of speed shown in 2014 were countered by moments of contact in a car that was less easy to drive than most. If Force India can produce a better handling car, this Mexican's class could yield even more fruit.

Look through this 25-year-old Mexican's career history and there is just one motor racing title to his name. That's not much compared to most of his F1 rivals, especially given that it's only for the National sub-class of the British Formula Three Championship. However, anyone who saw how he matched and often exceeded the pace of Force India team-mate Nico Hulkenberg last year, a driver with four car racing titles under his belt, will know that Sergio certainly has much to offer.

Sergio would assuredly have won titles in karting, but the Mexican motorsport body's decision to allow its young stars to step up to car racing at just 14 meant that he moved on when others were reaching the top of their game in karts. Nevertheless, Sergio gained valuable experience when he contested the Barber Dodge series in the United States of America.

When still only 15 years old, in 2005, he travelled to Europe to contest the German Formula BMW series. Staying on for a second year, he was given a taste of power late in the season when the Mexican A1GP team gave him an outing.

Sergio bounced back from being dropped by McLaren to show great speed.

Stepping up to Formula Three in 2007, Sergio won the National class title in the British series, then stayed on with T-Sport for 2008 and ranked fourth before rounding out the year in the Asian GP2 series.

A first full year in the main FIA GP2 Championship yielded two podium finishes in 2009 before he started winning in 2010, when racing for Arden International, and he not only ended the year as runner-up to Pastor Maldonado but had his first taste of F1 when he tested for Sauber.

The Swiss team was impressed enough to sign Sergio for 2011, and he rewarded them by scoring 14 points. He went better still to finish second in Malaysia in 2012, then had a year with McLaren that failed to hit the heights, with his best result for the team from Woking being fifth place in the Indian GP.

TRACK NOTES

Nationality:	MEXICAN
Born:	26 JANUARY 1990, GUADALAJARA, MEXICO
Website:	www.sergioperez.mx
Teams:	SAUBER 2011-12, McLAREN 2013, FORCE INDIA 2014-15

CAREER RECORD	
First Grand Prix:	2011 AUSTRALIAN GP
Grand Prix starts:	74
Grand Prix wins:	0 (best result: 2nd, 2012 Malaysian GP)
Poles:	0
Fastest laps:	3
Points:	188
Honours:	2010 GP2 RUNNER-UP, 2007 BRITISH FORMULA THREE NATIONAL CLASS CHAMPION

A YEAR OF PEAKS AND TROUGHS

When Sergio stood on the Sakhir podium after finishing third in the third of last year's 19 rounds, he would have been optimistic that he and Force India were all set for an outstanding season. The team had clearly got to grips with the new technical regulations better than many of their more esteemed rivals and had the good fortune to be running Mercedes V6 engines. This was cause for celebration for Sergio, who was feeling deflated after having been dropped by McLaren, but there were mechanical failures to keep him in check. Then came the Canadian GP, where his ability to preserve his tyres gave him a shot at victory, before his last lap clash with Felipe Massa. There was contact, too, in Hungary, when he got a wheel on a wet kerb and spun into the pitwall in a drive that was set to yield more points. Sadly, the Force India VJM07 became relatively less competitive thereafter until a late fillip for the final races, but Sergio proved a more robust character in 2014 and his obvious pace allied to great tyre management helped his star to shine brightly again.

NICO HULKENBERG

It's one of F1's mysteries why Nico is still not racing for one of the top teams. There was talk about his height and weight going against him as designers seek to make their cars tiny, but their loss is Force India's gain: he'll score every point on offer.

German junior kart champion at 15 in 2002, Nico won the senior title the following year. He didn't graduate to car racing until 2005 at the age of 17, but he made an instant impact by winning the Formula BMW ADAC Championship.

After a mixed German F3 Championship in 2006 when he shone in a less than competitive Ligier chassis against the predominant Dallaras, Nico impressed in a test and so became the lead driver for Germany's attack on the A1GP World Cup of Motorsport. He was the dominant driver and landed Germany the title, with his drive at a soaking wet Sepang being truly outstanding.

The European F3 Championship was his target for 2007 and he was the top rookie, winning four races to rank third overall for ASM as Romain Grosjean won the title. Nico had to make do with victory at the Masters F3 race at Zandvoort. Back for more in 2008, Nico was dominant champion, taking six wins for ART Grand Prix. The highlight of his year, though, was having his first taste of F1 by testing with Williams.

Staying with the same team, Nico stepped up to GP2 in 2009 and did

Having learned a lesson in preserving his rear tyres, Nico should be more effective still.

something that few have done before: he won the title as a rookie. Not only that, but he did it in style: his five wins left him fully 25 points clear of runner-up Vitaly Petrov and 64 points clear of his more experienced team-mate Pastor Maldonado.

Having undertaken more tests for Williams, Nico then signed for the team for 2010 and he rounded out that year with pole position in the wet in Brazil. Surplus to requirements in 2011, during which time he was reserve driver for Force India, Nico then raced for Force India in 2012, outscoring team-mate Paul di Resta, claiming fastest lap in Singapore and leading in Brazil. Moving to Sauber for 2013, he raced to a best finish of fourth, but advanced one place to rank 10th overall.

TRACK NOTES

Nationality:	GERMAN
Born:	19 AUGUST 1987, EMMERICH, GERMANY
Website:	www.nicohulkenberg.net
Teams:	WILLIAMS 2010, FORCE INDIA 2012, SAUBER 2013, FORCE INDIA 2014-15

CAREER RECORD

First Grand Prix:	2010 BAHRAIN GP
Grand Prix starts:	77
Grand Prix wins:	0 (best result: 4th, 2012 Belgian GP, 2013 Korean GP)
Poles:	1
Fastest laps:	1
Points:	232
Honours:	2009 GP2 CHAMPION, 2008 EUROPEAN FORMULA THREE CHAMPION, 2007 FORMULA THREEE MASTERS WINNER, 2006/07 A1GP CHAMPION, 2005 GERMAN FORMULA BMW ADAC CHAMPION & GERMAN FORMULA BMW RUNNER-UP, 2003 GERMAN KART CHAMPION, 2002 GERMAN JUNIOR KART CHAMPION

STARTING WITH A FLURRY

Nico's 2014 campaign with Force India was one of two halves. In the first half of the year, not only was he scoring points almost every race, but they were big helpings of points as he picked up four fifth-place finishes and two sixths in the first seven rounds. Indeed, after the third round, Nico ranked third overall. However, the VJM07 seemed not to develop in a way that suited the tall German, and team-mate Sergio Perez became the team's more potent tool for a while. Nico was left to continue scoring, but only with results in the bottom third of the top 10. He continued to drive with pace and intelligence, although he often seemed to be caught out by outside factors, such as the deployment of a safety car scuppering his tactics. There was a certain amount of on-track friction between himself and Perez, notably at the Bahrain GP, but that's only to be expected between two young drivers who are desperate to advance to racing for one of the top teams.

Dirtied from battle and forming probably the most expensive car park in the world, a selection of Formula One cars rest in the Interlagos Parc Ferme following the 2014 Brazilian Grand Prix.

SCUDERIA TORO ROSSO

Red Bull's junior team displayed flashes of speed last year, but this year's attack is all change – and all about youth. It will be intriguing to see how F1's youngest ever rookie pairing of Carlos Sainz Jr and 17-year-old Max Verstappen perform.

Scuderia Toro Rosso is starting afresh in 2015, with experienced hand Jean-Eric Vergne (above) being moved aside as two rookies are brought in.

Scuderia Toro Rosso has shown its relentless commitment to bring on young talent yet again by getting rid of one of its drivers from 2014. This time, despite outpacing his Red Bull Racing-bound team-mate Daniil Kvyat, Jean-Eric Vergne has been shown the door. Thus he joins a line of drivers who have fallen out of the Red Bull talent-search project to leave the way clear for a pair of even younger stars of the future: 20-year-old Carlos Sainz Jr and Max Verstappen.

The team was created in 2006 to act as a place for the best of Red Bull's many driver scholars to learn their craft and prove that they might be ready to step up to Red Bull Racing. This was the mastermind of Red Bull energy drinks magnate Dietrich Mateschitz and his sidekick Helmut Marko. Thus far, only Sebastian Vettel, Daniel Ricciardo and now Kvyat have made the big step.

Rather than start this team from scratch, Mateschitz bought Minardi. The Italian team founded by Fiat dealer Giancarlo Minardi began life in F2 in 1974, gradually making progress until Michele Alboreto won a round in 1981. Then, after F2 came to a close at the end of 1984 following a period of domination by Ralt, Minardi stepped up to F1 in 1985.

Always short of even an average budget, the team was a slow burner, with occasional flashes of speed, but largely spent each season competing just not to be last. By

THE POWER AND THE GLORY

FRANZ TOST
If Helmut Marko is the person responsible for picking the stars from Red Bull's junior programmes for Red Bull Racing, it's this Austrian team principal who nurtures that talent. Once an F3 racer, he turned to management when he took over the Walter Lechner Racing School in the 1980s. He then worked with Willi Weber in the 1990s, helping the Schumacher brothers, before joining Williams in 2000 to run its track operations. On the formation of Scuderia Toro Rosso from Minardi in 2006, he joined as team principal.

MOVING UP A POSITION
Toro Rosso advanced one place in the constructors' championship last year, demoting both Lotus and Sauber but losing out to Williams to end up seventh. While Jean-Eric Vergne put in some excellent performances, it was rookie Daniil Kvyat who caught most people's attention, overcoming his lack of experience by scoring in three of his first four races. Improved consistency in the second half of the season enabled the pair to operate just outside the top 10.

2014 DRIVERS & RESULTS

Driver	Nationality	Races	Wins	Pts	Pos
Jean-Eric Vergne	French	19	0	22	13th
Daniil Kvyat	Russian	19	0	8	15th

FOR THE RECORD

Country of origin:	Italy
Team base:	Faenza, Italy
Telephone:	(39) 546 696111
Website:	www.scuderiatororosso.com
Active in Formula One:	As Minardi 1985-2005
Grands Prix contested:	507
Wins:	1
Pole positions:	0
Fastest laps:	0

THE TEAM

Team owner:	Dietrich Mateschitz
Team principal:	Franz Tost
Technical director:	James Key
Deputy technical director:	Ben Waterhouse
Head of aerodynamics:	Brendan Gilhome
Head of vehicle performance:	
	Jody Egginton
Sporting director:	Graham Watson
Technical co-ordinator:	Sandro Parrini
Chief engineer:	Phil Charles
Test driver:	tba
Chassis:	Toro Rosso STR10
Engine:	Ferrari V6
Tyres:	Pirelli

1988, though, it had made it into the points, which were then awarded only to the top six finishers: Pierluigi Martini finished in sixth place in Detroit. The following season produced six points and Martini even led for a lap at Estoril. However, Minardi had to wait until 1990 for its greatest day when Martini qualified on the front row at Phoenix – this was due mainly to using Pirelli tyres that suited the conditions better than rival Goodyears. No points were scored that year.

Minardi soldiered on and could only weep in 1999 when Luca Badoer looked set for fourth at the Nürburgring until his gearbox broke. Three years later, Mark Webber nailed fifth place on his F1 debut with the team in Melbourne, but this wasn't enough to save the team and he moved on, to be replaced by drivers bringing money.

By 2006, Mateschitz had bought it and renamed the team as Scuderia Toro Rosso. For the first time, there was real money and things got better still in 2007: it ran the previous year's Red Bull chassis and Ferrari engines, and the arrival midseason of Sebastian Vettel in place of Scott Speed hinted at greater things.

Then in 2008, to everyone's amazement, Vettel mastered wet conditions at Monza. Not just in qualifying but when rain remained for the race and he stormed to victory. The team that had struggled as Minardi had now won on home ground. Red Bull was delighted, although it would have preferred RBR's own drivers to have achieved it. Indeed, it took them until 2009 to match this feat.

Since then, it has run a host of hopefuls, including Sebastien Bourdais, Jaime Alguersuari and Sebastien Buemi, but only two have been promoted to RBR: Ricciardo after edging out Vergne in 2013, and Kvyat being moved up to replace Ferrari-bound Vettel in 2014.

"With Carlos and Max in our driver line-up, we continue the Toro Rosso tradition of providing youngsters from the Red Bull Junior Driver Programme with their first steps in Formula One."

Franz Tost

Toro Rosso made its breakthrough at Monza in 2008, when Sebastian Vettel gave it its first win.

MAX VERSTAPPEN

If policemen appear to be getting ever younger, then so do F1 drivers: Max is the first 17-year-old to line up for a grand prix. The signs are that this second-generation racer is special, so it's small surprise that Scuderia Toro Rosso has signed him.

The son of Jos Verstappen is indeed a prodigy. No driver in the 65 years of F1 has reached the top of the sport by such a young age. Some will question whether Max can possibly be ready for F1 after just one year in car racing, but his speed and confidence were apparent each time he went out in an F1 car in 2014. This is why Scuderia Toro Rosso felt comfortable letting him drive one of its cars in the first practice session for the Japanese GP.

It must have helped to have Jos as a father as well as a kart-racing mother, Sophie Kumpen. The most valuable advice from Jos, though, will be about handling F1 at a young age: it's widely felt that Jos himself didn't achieve what he ought in F1 by reaching it too soon and thus not being mature enough to make the most of the opportunity. That said, it can't have helped to have Michael Schumacher as his Benetton team-mate in his first year ...

Max started in kart racing as soon as he was old enough to do so and his first title came in 2006, when he won the Belgian Rotax Minimax championship as he turned nine. He won the Dutch title the

Max will become F1's youngest ever driver when he makes his debut in Melbourne at 17.

following year. After adding more Dutch and Belgian titles, Max then made the step up to international karting in 2010, finishing second in the KF3 World Cup and winning the WSK World Series.

He capped his karting career in 2013 with title victories in the European KF and KZ Championships before landing the world's top karting prize, the World KZ title.

Not hanging around, he was encouraged by Jos to try out first Formula Renault and then Formula 3 cars before the year was out. As Max outpaced some of the established stars, it was clear that he was ready to go car racing.

What followed was a whirlwind, and Max would have ranked higher than third but for a run of early-season retirements.

TRACK NOTES

Nationality:	DUTCH
Born:	30 SEPTEMBER 1997, HASSELT, BELGIUM
Website:	www.verstappen.nl
Teams:	TORO ROSSO 2015

CAREER RECORD

First Grand Prix:	2015 AUSTRALIAN GP
Grand Prix starts:	0
Grand Prix wins:	0
Poles:	0
Fastest laps:	0
Points:	0
Honours:	2014 EUROPEAN FORMULA 3 RUNNER-UP, 2013 WORLD & EUROPEAN KZ KART CHAMPION & EUROPEAN KF KART CHAMPION, 2012 WSK MASTER SERIES KF2 CHAMPION, 2011 WSK EURO SERIES CHAMPION, 2010 WSK WORLD SERIES CHAMPION, 2009 BELGIAN KF5 CHAMPION, 2008 DUTCH CADET KART CHAMPION, 2007 & 2008 DUTCH MINIMAX CHAMPION, 2006 BELGIAN ROTAX MINIMAX CHAMPION

MAKING A MARK IN FORMULA 3

It's hard to believe that last year was Max's first in car racing. Yet, such is his youth, that this is indeed the case. He bypassed entry-level formulae such as Formula Renault and yet showed extraordinary speed when he started in the crack FIA European F3 Championship with Van Amersfoort Racing after a race-winning start in Ferrari's entry-level Florida Winter Series. Already qualifying on pole position by the second round, Max notched up his first win, then later won six races in a row to mount a title challenge against early-season pacesetter Esteban Ocon, who was racing for the more-fancied Prema Powerteam. He also won the standalone Masters event at Zandvoort. The Red Bull Junior Team then signed him up and suddenly Max's chances of promotion up through racing's categories became all the greater thanks to the finance that this scheme brings. Then, only a matter of days after his 17th birthday, he was offered the chance to show his skills when running the first practice session for Toro Rosso at the Japanese GP, in which he impressed.

CARLOS SAINZ JR

His father was two-time World Rally Champion, but it's the circuits that have always appealed more to Carlos Jr, and he now gets his chance this year with Scuderia Toro Rosso as one of a pair of rookies, of which he's the elder, at 20.

With Red Bull seeming to want its next batch of F1 hopefuls to be younger by the year, Carlos Jr knew that he couldn't afford to hang around last year. Contesting the Formula Renault 3.5 series, he knew that to stand a chance of being promoted to Red Bull's feeder team, Scuderia Toro Rosso, he had to become champion. And this he delivered, knowing that a way was opening up as Daniil Kvyat was being promoted to Red Bull Racing. Then, when Jean-Eric Vergne announced that he wasn't being kept on to be the experienced hand from whom 17-year-old Max Verstappen can learn, the way opened up and he was in.

With a father who was World Rally Champion, in both 1990 and 1992, and runner-up on four more occasions, you might have thought that Carlos Jr would take to the gravel stages out of preference, but he gained his first experience in karts at the age of seven, at an indoor circuit owned by his father and liked it. He didn't start competing until he was 11, winning the Madrid Cadet kart series, and that set him on course for a career in circuit racing.

Red Bull backing enabled Carlos Jr to move to cars at the age of 15, finishing

His father was World Rally Champion, but Carlos Jr has his sights set on F1 glory.

as the top-placed rookie in the European Formula BMW series, also winning the Asia-Pacific series round in Macau.

Advancing to Formula Renault with the Koiranen Motorsport team in 2011, he was runner-up to Robin Frijns in the European Formula Renault Championship, but won the lesser Northern European series.

Carlos Jr raced in Formula Three in 2012, ranking fifth in the European championship with the Carlin team. Then he tried GP3 in 2013, but showed good potential when he took in a few races in the more powerful Formula Renault 3.5 and experienced F1 power when testing with Toro Rosso, then Red Bull Racing.

For 2014, his was a full-time attack on Formula Renault 3.5, and it was what he did in this with the crack DAMS outfit that landed him his F1 break, as he won seven of the season's 17 rounds.

TRACK NOTES

Nationality:	SPANISH
Born:	1 SEPTEMBER 1994, MADRID, SPAIN
Website:	www.carlossainz.es
Teams:	TORO ROSSO 2015

CAREER RECORD

First Grand Prix:	2015 AUSTRALIAN GP
Grand Prix starts:	0
Grand Prix wins:	0
Poles:	0
Fastest laps:	0
Points:	0
Honours:	2014 FORMULA RENAULT 3.5 CHAMPION, 2011 EUROPEAN FORMULA RENAULT RUNNER-UP & NORTHERN EUROPEAN FORMULA RENAULT CHAMPION, 2009 MONACO KART CIUP WINNER, 2008 ASIA-PACIFIC JUNIOR KART CHAMPION, 2006 MADRID CADET KART CHAMPION

ONLY THE TITLE WOULD DO

Having tried a few Formula Renault 3.5 outings in 2013, Carlos Jr knew what to expect. Pole for the first race and victory in the second showed that he and the DAMS team were set for a good season. That breakthrough victory at Monza was followed up by one next time out, at Motorland Aragon, and then a brace at Spa-Francorchamps. A further win at the Nürburgring left him riding high, but there was then a disastrous meeting at the Hungaroring in which Roberto Mehri took a win and a second to cut into his advantage. Fortunately, Carlos Jr bounced back with a pair of wins at the penultimate meeting, at Paul Ricard, leaving him poised to take the title at the final round. This was at Jerez and the Spaniard's hopes of ending the year in style on home ground were scotched when he twice finished outside the top 10. But Mehri also failed to score and so he was able to hang on ahead of the winless but consistent Pierre Gasly.

LOTUS F1 TEAM

Few teams have started a season as short of testing as Lotus did last year and it spent the season trying to catch up. Once a title-winning team, a lack of budget and so a lack of certainty has reduced its prospects. This year, it has Mercedes engines.

Last year was a disaster for Lotus, but Romain Grosjean impressed as he pushed the E22 on. He and Maldonado will be hoping for better in 2015.

Some teams have changed their identity as they have welcomed in new finance and then gone on to greater things. This was once true of this team from Enstone, but its recent moves have seen it drop away rather than advance.

Having started life as Toleman in 1981, it came within a fraction of a second of winning the Monaco GP in 1984 when a race stoppage denied Ayrton Senna the chance to pass Alain Prost's McLaren. Renamed Benetton in 1986 after investment by the Italian knitwear manufacturer, it bounced back from a season without points to one in which it ranked sixth, Gerhard Berger winning the penultimate round, in Mexico. Fifth in 1987 was followed by third in 1988 as Thierry Boutsen and Alessandro Nannini racked up the points. The team was third again in 1990 through the best efforts of Nannini and Nelson Piquet, with the latter winning the final two rounds.

Titles continued to elude it as McLaren and then Williams kept it back, but two more third-placed seasons in 1992 and 1993 showed that it was ready for greater things. Part of this push was led by Michael Schumacher and he was the one, together with designer Rory Byrne and technical chief Ross Brawn, who gave it that final shove, edging out Williams' Damon Hill to land the 1994 drivers' title. Schumacher was champion again the

THE POWER AND THE GLORY

NICK CHESTER

The team's technical director since 2013, Nick has been with the team for 13 years since joining from Arrows. He began his career with Simtek Research, where he had worked on its shortlived F1 team. Nick then spent his early years with Lotus building up the team's simulation and analytical tools to develop its suspension, advancing to become engineering director after Genii Capital took over the team. In his spare time, which is rare, Nick races a C2 class sportscar in an historic championship for Group C cars.

GETTING IT WRONG FROM THE START

The team was woefully unprepared for last season and limped into the opening race in Australia, coming away with two retirements. However, the calibre of the team helped it to make up lost ground and Romain Grosjean put it in the points by the fifth round, with Pastor Maldonado getting close but not managing to get among the top 10 until round 17. Renault V6s weren't the engine of choice – Mercedes V6s were – but an increasing lack of finance was starting to show.

2014 DRIVERS & RESULTS

Driver	Nationality	Races	Wins	Pts	Pos
Romain Grosjean	French	19	0	8	14th
Pastor Maldonado	Venezuelan	19	0	2	16th

FOR THE RECORD

Country of origin:	England
Team base:	Enstone, England
Telephone:	(44) 01608 678000
Website:	www.lotusf1team.com
Active in Formula One:	As Toleman 1981-85, Benetton 1986-2001, Renault 2002-11
Grands Prix contested:	553
Wins:	48
Pole positions:	34
Fastest laps:	56

THE TEAM

Team principal:	Gerard Lopez
Chief executive officer:	Matthew Carter
Chief operating officer:	Thomas Mayer
Deputy team principal:	Federico Gastaldi
Technical director:	Nick Chester
Operations director:	Alan Permane
Chief designer:	Martin Tolliday
Head of aerodynamics:	Nicolas Hennel de Beaupreau
Team manager:	Paul Seaby
Chief mechanic:	Greg Baker
Race team co-ordinator:	Geoff Simmonds
Test driver:	Esteban Ocon
Chassis:	Lotus E23
Engine:	Mercedes V6
Tyres:	Pirelli

following year and the team landed the constructors' title thanks to Johnny Herbert adding two wins to Schumacher's nine.

On Schumacher's departure, Benetton welcomed back Berger and added fellow Ferrari leaver Jean Alesi for 1996. The team was pipped by Ferrari to be runner-up behind Williams. For 1998, Giancarlo Fisichella and Alexander Wurz took over, but Benetton faded over the next few years. Flavio Briatore returned in 2000 for a second spell as team principal and in 2002 the team changed its name for a second time, racing as Renault from 2002. This had no connection with the Renault team that had raced in F1 from 1977 to 1985. It was, in fact, more marketing-led – a factor that brought with it more finance, and Fernando Alonso was able to produce its first win at the Hungaroring in 2003. The team then went from strength to strength as Jarno Trulli won at Monaco in 2004, then Fisichella got in on the act in Melbourne in 2005 before Alonso raced to his first drivers' title. Renault also landed the constructors' title that year and in 2006.

Since then, the going has never been so good. Robert Kubica promised great things, but his F1 career was curtailed by injuries suffered when contesting a rally in 2011.

Renamed as Lotus Renault GP for 2012, the team headed towards another change when it became Lotus F1 Team in 2013. Again, there is no connection with the original Lotus team, or indeed with the Team Lotus created by Tony Fernandes in 2010. It was fourth in both 2012 and 2013, with Kimi Raikkonen winning in Abu Dhabi in 2012 and in Australia in 2013, backed up ably by Romain Grosjean.

For 2015, Maldonado will stay on, his backing from Venezuela still a help. Grosjean had hoped that his increasingly strong and consistent form would have landed him a drive with a front-running outfit, but last year's awful results put paid to that. Mercedes engines should be a big boost.

"Towards the end of last year, some of the things that we did on the car were designed for us to learn for 2015. It was worth switching focus, as it allowed us to try more things before changing to the Mercedes power unit."
Nick Chester

Back when the team was Benetton, Michael Schumacher celebrates winning the 1994 European GP.

ROMAIN GROSJEAN

Romain is a driver who has proved his talent over the past few seasons and now needs a set of wheels with which to shine, something that the Lotus team patently failed to supply him with last year. Mercedes engines should be a huge help.

Although Romain hasn't won a top-level international single-seater race for four years, his last win coming in GP2 at the Hungaroring in 2011, he was always a champion in every category until he reached F1, so he must be fretting that this, his fourth full season at the sport's top level, really needs to be the one in which he becomes a grand prix winner at last.

Of course, the majority of drivers who make it to F1 never manage to make this last step, but Romain is better than most and deserves a car good enough to take a tilt at winning. In 2015, that means for a second year running that he needs to be in a Mercedes, which he isn't, but a Mercedes-powered Lotus will surely be a more potent package than he had last year when his E22 was fitted with the less competitive Renault power unit.

Look at Romain's career and there are very few drivers who can match his record of being champion in so many different categories: Formula Renault 1600, then Formula Renault, Formula Three, GP2 and Auto GP. Not surprisingly, he has faith in his ability and backs his own talent: he stepped back to lesser formulae in 2010 after he

Romain matured in 2014 as he faced a character-building year and might yet surprise in 2015.

failed to secure the offer of a contract extension following his part-season of F1 in 2009 with Renault when he took over Nelson Piquet Jr's ride for the final seven rounds. He then got his head down and won the Auto GP title, as well as winning a couple of FIA GT1 races in a Matech Ford GT. Winning the GP2 title in 2011 was essential, and earned him his ticket back to F1.

Yes, Romain was wild when he returned to F1, with some of his misdemeanors in 2012 making other drivers not want to run near him, but he does appear to have learnt from them.

For the record, Romain's last victory anywhere was in the multi-discipline Race of Champions in 2012, when he beat Tom Kristensen in Bangkok after they beat Michael Schumacher and David Coulthard respectively to reach the final.

TRACK NOTES

Nationality:	FRENCH
Born:	17 APRIL 1986, GENEVA, SWITZERLAND
Website:	www.romaingrosjean.com
Teams:	RENAULT 2009, LOTUS 2012-15

CAREER RECORD	
First Grand Prix:	2009 EUROPEAN GP
Grand Prix starts:	64
Grand Prix wins:	0
	(best result: 2nd, 2012 Canadian GP, 2013 United States GP)
Poles:	0
Fastest laps:	1
Points:	236
Honours:	2011 GP2 CHAMPION & GP2 ASIA CHAMPION, 2010 AUTO GP CHAMPION, 2008 GP2 ASIA CHAMPION, 2007 FORMULA THREE EUSOSERIES CHAMPION, 2005 FRENCH FORMULA RENAULT CHAMPION, 2003 SWISS FORMULA RENAULT 1600 CHAMPION

A SEASON SPENT CHASING

There is no word other than "disastrous" to describe Lotus' performance at last year's opening round. The team simply wasn't ready for the new technical regulations and the following three flyaway grands prix were just a case of hanging on. Yet, the team is too good to stay down and at least made steps in time for the Spanish GP. Romain responded with eighth place, then did the same in Monaco. Yet, while the shortage of horsepower from its Renault V6s was one problem, the chassis behaviour was even more of an issue, and so bad was the combined situation that the team did right to swing its focus early on to 2015. It was frustrating for the drivers, with Romain the more concerned of the pair because he doesn't come with the millions in sponsorship that Pastor Maldonado does, but his input and the team's recall of the second place finishes that he achieved in each of 2012 and 2013 were enough to ensure that he was signed for another year.

Last year was the greatest disappointment of Pastor's racing career. He believed that he was leaving Williams to join a team at the sharp end of the grid and found, instead, that he had gone backwards. So, 2015 is of considerable importance.

After three years in karting, Pastor moved from Venezuela at the age of 18 in 2003 to pursue his car racing ambitions. Based in Italy, he raced for Cram Competition in Formula Renault.

Having ranked seventh in the Italian championship, he returned in 2004 and won the crown. He also tested himself by entering the European Championship and he won the season's opening pair of races at Monza. He didn't win again, though, so ended up eighth overall as Scott Speed won the title.

Seeking more power, Pastor raced in both the World Series by Renault and the Italian F3000 series in 2005, scoring a win in the latter. In 2006, he focused on the World Series by Renault for the Draco team, and ranked third.

The final stepping stone to F1, GP2, was next and Pastor won a race at Monaco for Trident Racing but ranked only 11th after an inconsistent campaign. He also contested Euroseries F3000 rounds and won one of the two races he entered. Returning to go for the title in 2008, Pastor was again a winner, at Spa-Francorchamps, but he

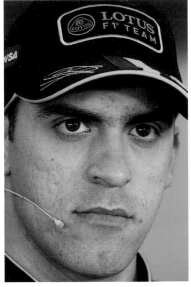

Pastor will have watched former team Williams with frustration but will want to challenge again.

disappointed by ending the year only fifth.

He chose to return for a third year of GP2, which isn't seen as a good thing to do because it suggests a driver who is not ready for F1. This time Pastor drove with

ART Grand Prix - and suffered the ignominy of ranking only sixth as his rookie team-mate Nico Hulkenberg claimed the title. Then, having one last crack at GP2 in 2010, Pastor landed the title at last, winning six races for Rapax.

His sizeable sponsorship package landed him his F1 break with Williams in 2011 and, after scoring a point, he delivered a peerless drive to victory in the 2012 Spanish GP. This feat, though, was the exception to the rule and Pastor's on-track disciplinary record continued to show that his speed was counterbalanced by recklessness.

There was no love last between Pastor and Williams by the end of 2013, so he moved on to Lotus.

AN EXTREMELY DIFFICULT YEAR

Seldom has an established team turned up in such disarray for the opening round of a season as Lotus did last year. The E22 was woefully short of running when it arrived at Albert Park and its initial runs in practice were hampered by numerous failures. This was a major setback to Pastor, who had quit Williams with high hopes to drive for the team that ranked fourth in 2013. Although his team-mate Romain Grosjean did manage the occasional point-scoring drive through 2014, the Venezuelan remained outside the top 10 until the 17th of the season's 19 rounds. The team was short on finance to develop the car, so there was no late-season surge into the points and Pastor's feelings of frustration were palpable - no doubt made worse by seeing his former team become one of the leading challengers. However, with financial backing still behind him, Pastor knew that he was at least likely to remain in F1 for 2015, a luxury that Grosjean couldn't bank on. After all, a team needs money to fund the perpetual development required to stay in the hunt.

TRACK NOTES

Nationality:	VENEZUELAN
Born:	9 MARCH 1985, MARACAY, VENEZUELA
Website:	www.pastormaldonado.com
Teams:	WILLIAMS 2011-13, LOTUS 2014-15

CAREER RECORD

First Grand Prix:	2011 AUSTRALIAN GP
Grand Prix starts:	77
Grand Prix wins:	1
	2012 Spanish GP
Poles:	1
Fastest laps:	0
Points:	49
Honours:	2010 GP2 CHAMPION, 2004 ITALIAN FORMULA RENAULT CHAMPION, 2003 ITALIAN FORMULA RENAULT WINTER SERIES CHAMPION

Pastor Maldonado's Lotus is launched by contact with Esteban Gutierrez's Sauber at the British GP, but it was Gutierrez who retired.

SAUBER

This is a team that took a tumble last year and failed to score a single championship point. For 2015, still without a new major shareholder to bring much needed finance, Sauber needs to start its programme of re-establishing itself in the midfield.

New season, new drivers for Sauber, as both Esteban Gutierrez (above) and Adrian Sutil make way for Marcus Ericsson and Felipe Nasr.

Formed in 1993 from a sportscar team set up by Peter Sauber, it has won just once, in 2008, and often been a solidly midfield outfit. However, last year showed that the lack of the giant budget required by the top teams is holding it back.

Peter Sauber was a sportscar racer of note, but his name rose higher when he turned to building Group C sportscars. The way that his sports-prototypes ran with Mercedes power impressed Mercedes so much that they went into partnership, with Peter running the works entries from 1988, winning the teams' and drivers' titles in 1989 and 1990 plus the 1989 Le Mans 24 Hours.

F1 was next, although Mercedes pulled out of the deal, leaving Sauber to enter the World Championship in 1993 with Ilmor power. JJ Lehto finished fifth on the team's debut at Kyalami and Sauber ended the year an impressive equal sixth with Lotus, helped by Lehto claiming fourth at Imola and Karl Wendlinger another fourth at Monza.

Heinz-Harald Frentzen replaced Lehto for 1994. That year, Wendlinger placed fourth at Imola, but in the following race at Monaco, he crashed and spent three weeks in a coma.

Ford power replaced Mercedes motors in 1996 and Frentzen finished third at Monza, but the team made no progress. Nor did it burst out of the midfield in 1997, when

THE POWER AND THE GLORY

GIAMPAOLO DALL'ARA
Giampaolo Dall'ara has a lengthy history with Sauber, having moved to the Swiss team back in 2000. Before that, he worked at Fiat's research centre in Turin, focusing on handling development, and he then started working on Alfa Romeo's programme in the International Touring Car Championship. A three-year spell followed with Alfa Romeo's Supertouring team before he moved to F1 with Sauber. Starting as an engineer for the test team, Giampaolo became a race engineer, then senior strategist and now head of track engineering.

A FRUITLESS QUEST FOR POINTS
Last year was an immensely frustrating one for Sauber: it always seemed to end up just outside the points despite the best efforts of Adrian Sutil and Esteban Gutierrez. Not only was their Ferrari V6 no match for the teams using Mercedes and Renault V6s, but they both suffered assorted reliability problems. This began to worry the team when Jules Bianchi finished ninth at Monaco to move Marussia ahead in the rankings and thus land a larger share of the prize money.

2014 DRIVERS & RESULTS

Driver	Nationality	Races	Wins	Pts	Pos
Adrian Sutil	German	19	0	0	18th
Esteban Gutierrez	Mexican	19	0	0	20th

FOR THE RECORD

Country of origin:	Switzerland
Team base:	Hinwil, Switzerland
Telephone:	(41) 44 937 9000
Website:	www.sauberf1team.com
Active in Formula One:	From 1993
	(as BMW Sauber 2006-10)
Grands Prix contested:	383
Wins:	1
Pole positions:	1
Fastest laps:	5

THE TEAM

Team principal:	Monisha Kaltenborn
Operations director:	Axel Kruse
Chief designer:	Eric Gandelin
Head of aerodynamics:	Willem Toet
Head of vehicle performance:	
	Elliot Dason-Barber
Head of track engineering:	
	Giampaolo Dall'ara
Head of track operations:	Otmar Bartsch
Team manager:	Beat Zehnder
Test driver:	Raffaele Marciello
Chassis:	Sauber C34
Engine:	Ferrari V6
Tyres:	Pirelli

a deal was done to run Ferrari customer engines, although Johnny Herbert did come third in Hungary. The team then settled into ranking eighth for the next few years until it leapt to fourth in 2001, a year that Michael Schumacher dominated for Ferrari. Nick Heidfeld and rookie Kimi Raikkonen both impressed, with Heidfeld's third in Brazil its best result, with two fourths from the Finn.

After ranking fifth in 2002, Frentzen returned to pick up a surprise third at Indianapolis in 2003, and Giancarlo Fisichella and Felipe Massa picked up a fourth place apiece in 2004. Massa claimed another fourth in 2005, as did Jacques Villeneuve, but it took the arrival of a partnership with BMW in 2006 to move things forward again.

For the next four years, the team would race as BMW Sauber, and the German manufacturer had picked its moment well. The F1.07 was competitive in 2007 and, combined with BMW's V8, it powered the team towards the front, Heidfeld and Robert Kubica helping the team finish as distant runners-up

to Ferrari – the team's best result second in Canada. The team then scored its only win thus far, in 2008, when Kubica led Heidfeld home in a surprise one-two in Montreal.

Being based in rural Switzerland has always held Sauber back because attracting the services of the predominantly British designers and engineers who dominate F1 remains a struggle.

Monisha Kaltenborn took the reins in 2012, when Sauber stepped back from the frontline. Talk about the team being taken over by a syndicate of Russians before last season came to naught, and last autumn there was much speculation that a dual-purpose deal might be done by Canadian fashion tycoon Lawrence Stroll. He has long wanted an F1 team, having been involved in Lotus when it folded in 1994, but he now has a second reason. His 16-year-old son Lance is a hot prospect in F3, already signed to Ferrari's Young Driver programme, and this team could offer Lance a way into F1. Stroll Sr's first involvement with Ferrari was in the

1990s, when the team was backed by Tommy Hilfiger, a fashion brand he managed. At the time of writing, no deal has been completed.

New money, plus that from incoming racers Marcus Ericsson and Felipe Nasr, will be welcome, but don't expect a sudden turnaround – such things can take years.

Nick Heidfeld and Robert Kubica battle for the lead at the 2008 Canadian GP in Montreal, when Kubica gave BMW Sauber its only win.

⊕ MARCUS ERICSSON

This Swedish racer didn't arrive in F1 last year as a driver expected to set the world on fire, but he set to the task of learning the ropes with financially beleaguered Caterham and impressed increasingly as he advanced through the year.

Marcus took a long time to prove himself in F1's feeder formula, GP2. Four years, in fact, so no one viewed him as an overnight sensation when he finally reached F1 with Caterham last year.

Trying a kart at the age of nine, Marcus had the good fortune that the track was owned by Swedish touring car racer Fredrik Ekblom, who recognized some nascent talent and so urged Marcus's father to buy him a kart. When he was old enough to transfer to car racing, Marcus was guided towards Fortec Motorsport by Ekblom and another of the team's former charges, Kenny Brack.

The involvement of the latter was important: this fellow Swede, the F3000 runner-up in 1996 and Indycar champion in 1998, has helped Marcus ever since.

54

The British Formula BMW Championship in 2007 was the first step and Marcus came on strong to win the final four races to land the title. In the 2008 British F3 Championship in 2008, when Jaime Alguersuari swept to the title, he ranked fifth for Fortec before accepting a drive from TOM's to contest the Japanese F3 series in 2009. This move paid off, and so

Marcus came on well with Caterham and brought his backers with him to join Sauber.

he claimed his second car racing title.

GP2 was next, joining another of Brack's old teams, Super Nova. After contesting a few races in GP2 Asia at the end of 2009, he moved on to the FIA

series in 2010. A winner at Valencia, he was erratic, however, and ranked only 17th.

A change of team to iSport advanced Marcus to 10th overall in 2011 before he won a race at Spa-Francorchamps in 2012 to help him rank eighth.

Few drivers return for a fourth year in GP2, but Marcus did, this time with DAMS. Realistically, only the title would do if he was to going to realize his dream of reaching F1, but Marcus was able to offer only a win at the Nürburgring en route to ranking sixth overall in a series won by Fabio Leimer. However, strong backing from Sweden enabled Marcus to buy the second seat at financially struggling Caterham and so he managed to reach the World Championship stage.

MAKING PROGRESS IN YEAR ONE

Driving for Caterham in 2014 was never going to result in a flurry of points, and this indeed proved to be the case, 11th place in the incident-packed race at Monaco being the closest that Marcus got. Through the first half of the season, he lagged behind team-mate Kamui Kobayashi, but then the Swedish F1 rookie started to make progress, out-qualifying his more experienced Japanese rival and, as the season drew to a close, outracing him too. Marcus's speed is not – never has been – in doubt, but his judgement certainly is, as shown by various on-track incidents in his career. These continued last year, and included crashing in Hungary and spinning behind the safety car in Japan. Commendably, though, Marcus began to string together performances that were close to extracting the maximum from the admittedly limited Renault-engined Caterham CT05, especially in Singapore. So, armed with the healthy financial package that has been a feature of his career thus far, he ought to do better still with Sauber in 2015.

TRACK NOTES

Nationality:	SWEDISH
Born:	2 SEPTEMBER 1990, KUMLA, SWEDEN
Website:	www.marcusericsson.com
Teams:	CATERHAM 2014, SAUBER 2015

CAREER RECORD

First Grand Prix:	2014 AUSTRALIAN GP
Grand Prix starts:	16
Grand Prix wins:	0 (best result: 11th, 2014 Monaco GP)
Poles:	0
Fastest laps:	0
Points:	0
Honours:	2009 JAPANESE FORMULA 3 CHAMPION, 2007 BRITISH FORMULA BMW CHAMPION

FELIPE NASR

Completing the wholesale change of Sauber's driver line-up, Felipe steps up to F1 after proving his worth across three years of GP2. He brings with him the experience of some F1 test runs with Williams as well as much-needed backing from Brazil.

Felipe comes from a family steeped in motor racing, his uncle Amir Nasr long being a frontrunner in Brazilian F3, so it came as no surprise that Felipe started racing karts as soon as he was old enough.

In 2007, when he was 15, he took the Brazilian Karting Championship title. Amir then ran Felipe in the final two races of the 2008 Formula BMW Americas championship when the series visited Interlagos, and he landed an impressive third place in the second of these on his car racing debut.

Making the most of this experience, Felipe headed for Europe and won the 2009 Formula BMW Europe Championship title at a canter. Stepping up to F3 in 2010, he won once and ranked fifth overall in the British championship for Raikkonen Robertson Racing as Jean-Eric Vergne powered to the title.

Moving across to Vergne's old team, Carlin, Felipe then scored seven wins in 2011 to become champion ahead of Kevin Magnussen, also finishing second in Macau's end-of-year F3 street race.

Graduating to GP2 for 2012, Felipe had high hopes, but his season with DAMS

Felipe has racked up good F1 mileage with Williams and is desperate to perform for Brazil.

yielded four podium finishes but no wins, leaving him 10th overall as his team-mate Davide Valsecchi became champion.

Back with Carlin for 2013, Felipe did everything but win a race, finishing on the podium six times en route to ranking

fourth at year's end as Fabio Leimer took the spoils.

Clearly, this wasn't enough to give him a boost into F1, but Felipe wished to continue with his F1 dream, so he had to come back for a third crack at F1's feeder formula in 2014. Fortunately, he did enough to finish the year as GP2 runner-up (see below) and then, armed with sponsorship from Banco do Brasil, landed one of the two Sauber seats for 2015 as the team's 2014 racers Adrian Sutil and Esteban Gutioerrez were eased aside.

Felipe can only hope that the Swiss team can produce a better car/engine package than it did in 2014 if he is to emulate former racing rival Magnussen and score points in his rookie season.

TRACK NOTES

Nationality:	BRAZILIAN
Born:	21 AUGUST 1992, BRASILIA, BRAZIL
Website:	www.felipenasr.com
Teams:	SAUBER 2015

CAREER RECORD

First Grand Prix:	2015 AUSTRALIAN GP
Grand Prix starts:	0
Grand Prix wins:	0
Poles:	0
Fastest laps:	0
Points:	0
Honours:	2014 GP2 RUNNER-UP, 2011 BRITISH FORMULA 3 CHAMPION, 2009 FORMULA BMW EUROPE CHAMPION, 2007 BRAZILIAN KARTING CHAMPION

FROM WINNER TO F1 DRIVER

Contesting a third year of GP2 was a career risk for 2014, but Felipe hadn't shown quite enough in the previous two campaigns – ranking 10th and then fourth overall – to merit his promotion to an F1 race seat. What he had to do above all else was to start winning races again. And this Felipe did, reaching the top step of a GP2 podium for the first time at the second round, at the Circuit de Catalunya. With further wins following at the Red Bull Ring, Silverstone and Spa-Francorchamps, he strayed into the title fight, but his 2013 team-mate Jolyon Palmer was on even better form for DAMS and was able to keep scoring consistently enough to wrap up the title before the final round. By winning races, though, Felipe had removed any question marks about his talent. This was then backed up by some impressive runs for Williams in the first Friday practice at several grands prix, and all the experience gained from these made him look ready for the final challenge.

Formula One offers lows as well as highs: Kamui
Kobayashi's season got off to a first-corner fumble
at the Australian GP, and the Caterham team made it to
the final round only after asking fans for contributions.

TALKING POINT: TEAMS STRUGGLE AS COSTS KEEP RISING

It's always news when an F1 team fails, and two stumbled in 2014, but this has been a constant in F1's history. Right now, though, F1 has become too expensive for its own good and answers are needed for its survival.

The six-and-a-half decades of the Formula 1 World Championship haven't been one long, smooth ride. There have been periods when the grids have thinned and others, such as the late 1980s, when there have been so many cars turning up that not only is qualifying required but pre-qualifying too to sort the fastest 26 cars to put onto the grid.

It's abundantly clear, though, that as the global economy attempts to pull itself out of its downturn F1 is hitting another thin patch. Last year's World Championship started out with 11 teams, and thus 22 cars, and looked set to end with just nine teams. Only an administrator taking the reins of Caterham bolstered the numbers back to 10 for the final round thanks to a crowdfunding appeal. This certainly didn't show F1 in the best light, leaving the World Championship looking in need of repair.

One problem that has been around since Alfa Romeo steamrollered all opposition at the first ever World Championship round, at Silverstone in 1950, is that there have always been the haves and the have nots. Or, given today's stratospheric costs and giant teams with many hundreds of personnel, the ultra rich and the almost rich. It's hard not to feel that the sport has reached a point at which something has to be done, or the number of teams will dwindle further.

It's not just Caterham and Marussia that struggled through 2014. The next teams up the ladder – Sauber, Force India and Lotus – talked of boycotting last November's US GP in protest at the lack of help they felt they were getting from F1's owners, CVC Capital Partners, in keeping costs in check.

They pointed out that their engine bill was now 70% of their budget, and that what was left was no longer sufficient for them to design and build their cars and then run them in 20 rounds.

As they puzzled about their financial survival, there was a clear danger that the remaining teams would have to run more than two cars each in order for F1 to keep the number of cars up to its contractual minimum of 20. Otherwise the FIA could step in and take control. No team wanted a third car, for reasons both of cost and because no third car would be eligible for points. Fortunately, FIA president Jean Todt said last December that he saw no need for pushing for third cars, even if numbers dropped below 20, especially as the Haas team is due to make its debut in 2016.

Three-car teams aren't something new, though. Indeed, Alfa Romeo fielded four at Silverstone in the spring of 1950. In the 1970s, McLaren ran two cars in Marlboro livery, for Emerson Fittipaldi and Denny Hulme, while it also ran a third car in Yardley livery for Mike Hailwood. March, at that time, would run all of its cars in different colour schemes. At its launch in 1999, BAR had no plans to run three cars, but intended for its pair to run in different liveries. This was immediately quashed and it was stressed that uniformity of livery had become one of F1's rules.

One solution to dwindling numbers suggested last autumn was running a sub-class of cars, sort of GP2 plus. This happened last in 1987, when there was a separate Jim Clark Cup for cars run with normally aspirated engines as turbos took over. However, that was soon dismissed.

Another approach could be the purchasing of chassis from the top teams, but the long-term effect could be to scupper the midfield teams. It's likely that their best efforts wouldn't be enough to beat these bought chassis, thus pushing them down the rankings and, crucially, the prize-money list. To propel established racing constructors to the drop would certainly not be in the interest of the sport. If they crumbled, and then one of the manufacturers felt that it had extracted all it wanted from F1, there would be a grave danger of F1 being left without a decent grid of cars now that the long-standing racing constructors had been forced out. Lose the constructors, and you lose the sport's identity and open the way for spec cars, the fastest route to proving that excellence no longer matters, thus blunting motor racing's sharpest tool.

New measures, such as a cap on budgets, something that is always difficult when manufacturers are involved, seem more necessary now than ever.

Right: Marcus Ericsson is congratulated by his Caterham crew. The team struggled to complete 2014 and needs considerable backing to survive.

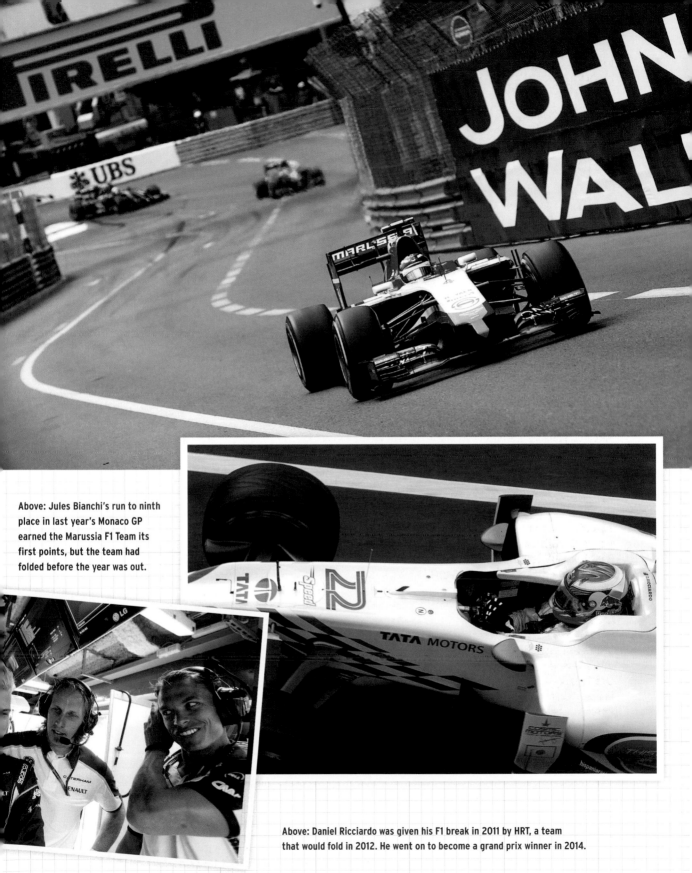

Above: Jules Bianchi's run to ninth place in last year's Monaco GP earned the Marussia F1 Team its first points, but the team had folded before the year was out.

Above: Daniel Ricciardo was given his F1 break in 2011 by HRT, a team that would fold in 2012. He went on to become a grand prix winner in 2014.

TALKING POINT:
F1'S CENTRES OF EXCELLENCE
ARE CENTRED ON ENGLAND

When the World Championship began in 1950, Italian teams dominated the sport. Then Germany flexed its muscles before a British revolution in design in the late 1950s saw the engine moved to behind the driver. Since then, England has been home to almost all of the teams' high-tech HQs.

With up to 600 staff, F1 teams require a lot of space, and the ingredients that they all need include a state-of-the-art design office, a wind tunnel, CAD/CAM production facilities, a composites department, an electronics division, a simulator, shaker rigs to work through set-up data on a grand prix weekend and bays for their race transporters. None of this comes cheap, but some teams can make money by having divisions that work on technology applicable to the automotive industry, such as Williams's work on hybrid technology.

The most impressive aspect of all is just how beautiful these team HQs are. They are often sleek architectural buildings with manufacturing facilities that are as clean as operating theatres. That's a far cry from only a few decades ago when they were often converted industrial units with supplementary sections added on as their needs changed, with oily rags to be found alongside grubby preparation bays.

The location of a team HQ is as important as the facilities it has. Teams need to employ highly skilled staff and these are not to be found scattered everywhere, but instead are concentrated in pockets of engineering excellence. Ferrari is (unsurprisingly) located in Italy. Based in Maranello, it even has a test circuit of its own, Fiorano, just behind the factory that builds its road cars. Yet, F1's most successful team is very much in a minority because it is not based in England. In fact, there was a time in the late 1980s when Ferrari's British design chief John Barnard insisted its design team operated out of Guildford in Surrey – a

demand that caused friction for implying the Italian team didn't have the expertise to hit F1's highest notes. After Barnard left, all focus returned to Italy, but even with the opening of an all-new HQ that will help to streamline its sporting activities on a site which used to contain 45 buildings, F1's powerbase remains in Britain.

Williams is as British as they come, so it is no surprise that its headquarters are in Oxfordshire. Furthermore, although McLaren was founded by New Zealander Bruce McLaren, it has always been based in England, first near Heathrow and now in the most remarkable technical centre of excellence of all, outside Woking.

Red Bull Racing is listed as Austrian, since Austria is the home of the product and the man who created it. Yet its base is not in an Alpine valley but instead in Milton Keynes. Indeed, it's the one-time home of Stewart GP before it became Jaguar Racing and then Red Bull in 2005.

Anyone new to F1 would make a guess that Mercedes GP must be based in Germany. Yet the team is based in Brackley, just west of Silverstone, rather than near the automotive manufacturer's global headquarters in Stuttgart. Brackley is where the old BAR team based itself before the 1999 season, wanting to be close to the designers, engineers, technicians and parts suppliers that are grouped in an arc that starts south-west of London, in Surrey, then runs north towards Oxford and east to Peterborough. BAR itself became Honda Racing, then Brawn GP, before assuming its latest identity as Mercedes GP in 2010.

Likewise, Force India doesn't operate from India. The team that was first Jordan, then Midland, then Spyker, has its factory opposite the main entrance at Silverstone. Lotus, known formerly as Toleman, Benetton and Renault, is also located near Silverstone, at Enstone, while Marussia's base was up the road at Banbury and Caterham occupied the old Arrows headquarters at Leafield.

Ferrari isn't alone in operating from outside Britain, though, as two other teams do the same. Also in Italy, Scuderia Toro Rosso calls Faenza home, just as the team from which it sprang in 2006 – Minardi – did. Sauber, though, has always been a Swiss team, based at Hinwil. This has made it hard to employ the staff it requires, as many designers and engineers don't want to uproot their families from England or from northern Italy.

When Team US F1 aimed to join the World Championship in 2010, it elected to base itself in the USA. Likewise, Gene Haas's team, pencilled in to join the show in 2016, has also named an American location for its base. Some might say that Haas is putting national pride too high up on his agenda, but he's determined that American engineers will be up to the task.

Right: Mercedes-Benz is a German manufacturer, but the team is based in England, at Brackley, just a few miles to the west of Silverstone.

Left: McLaren's Technology Centre provides the perfect backdrop for launches. This is from 2013, when Sergio Perez joined Jenson Button on the driving force.

Below: Red Bull Racing operates from Milton Keynes, in the heart of F1's arc around London.

TALKING POINT: SHOULD TEAM ORDERS HAVE A PLACE IN FORMULA ONE?

Team orders have existed almost since the dawn of motor racing. However, they have often been unpopular with both drivers and fans alike, as well as the media, and drivers sometimes simply ignore them, guaranteeing a more than frosty atmosphere on the podium after the race.

It wasn't always like this. Take 1956, when Ferrari's Peter Collins was happy to pull over and cede his car to Juan Manuel Fangio at the Italian GP, when his team leader's machine failed. This cost him the title, and clinched it for Fangio, but the 24-year-old Englishman reasoned that he'd have other opportunities once the 45-year-old Argentinian had retired. Sadly, Collins was killed before his dreams could be realized. Back then, cars broke down regularly and it was considered normal for a junior driver to hand over their car.

Two decades later, attitudes to team orders had changed. Loyalty, and perhaps an eye on the future, were probably why Ronnie Peterson agreed to be number two to Mario Andretti at Lotus in 1978, when Colin Chapman brought him back to the team he had left at the start of 1977. With its lead in ground effects aerodynamics, Lotus was on top and the mercurial Swede was content to defer to Andretti as the American edged closer to the title. Then, awfully, Peterson crashed at the start of the Italian GP and died of his injuries.

From time to time, and often when a team has a performance advantage, a pre-race agreement gets put in place. This is largely to avoid team-mates colliding at the first corner, but it has backfired. McLaren's Ayrton Senna and Alain Prost disagreed about the interpretation of a pre-race deal at Imola in 1989, saying that whoever led into the first corner wouldn't be attacked. Prost duly led into Tamburello, but Senna passed him anyway later at Tosa. This ignited the simmering feud between the two men.

Nine years later, at the Australian GP, another pre-race agreement surfaced, when Mika Hakkinen pitted when McLaren wasn't expecting him in – he'd misheard a bogus message from someone who'd hacked into their radio system. Team-mate David Coulthard agreed to slow down and let the Finn catch up, as they'd stated that whoever led into the first corner would win. Many drivers might not have bothered.

Of course, having team orders when one driver is faster makes sense in case the lead driver has been slowed by a problem and needs his number two to let him past as he recovers. This becomes less easy to stomach when the number two is ahead on merit. Ferrari messes with this the most, as shown when Michael Schumacher was all but unstoppable as he gathered five drivers' titles in a row from 2000. A low point came at the 2002 Austrian GP when Rubens Barrichello was told to hand victory to Schumacher. He did so, between the final corner on the last lap and the finish. This infuriated the crowd in what was, after all, only the sixth round of a 17-round campaign. The FIA responded by banning team orders.

This problem occurred again in the 2010 German GP when team leader Fernando Alonso had no answer to Felipe Massa's pace. Ferrari wanted the Spaniard ahead, though, so told the Brazilian to back off. It was demeaning. Many were amazed when, after fining Ferrari $100,000, the FIA elected to permit team orders again, saying they were "difficult to detect and police".

In between, in 2007, Lewis Hamilton claimed that he'd been instructed to remain behind McLaren team-mate Alonso in the Monaco GP. This was a vague situation, as McLaren hadn't asked Alonso to let him by, but also hadn't allowed Hamilton to push.

At Sepang in 2013, Sebastian Vettel infuriated team-mate Mark Webber by ignoring Red Bull's "Multi 21" instruction to remain behind the Australian, who'd followed orders and backed his engine off to save it.

Most recently, Hamilton was furious when asked by Mercedes GP team chief Paddy Lowe to let Nico Rosberg through in 2014's Hungarian GP, despite starting from the pits, enduring a spin on the opening lap and still advancing to third place. Lowe wasn't deliberately favouring points leader Rosberg, but an analysis of likely speed convinced him that Rosberg stood a chance of passing both Alonso and Daniel Ricciardo to win, and Hamilton did not. Hamilton said: "I'm not letting him past. If he gets close enough to overtake, he can overtake me." Mercedes GP's non-executive chairman Niki Lauda, ever a racer, came out in support of Hamilton.

As most drivers are employees, though, they have to expect to be told what to do.

Top right: When Juan Manuel Fangio's Ferrari failed in the 1956 Italian GP, team-mate Peter Collins (26) handed over his car.

Centre left: Lewis Hamilton and Nico Rosberg fought for supremacy last year, which made for some awkward press conferences.

Centre right: After Rubens Barrichello let him by in Austria in 2002, Michael Schumacher was so embarrassed that he put the Brazilian onto the top step of the podium.

Bottom right: Alain Prost leads away from Ayrton Senna at Imola in 1989, but the McLaren drivers' positions were soon reversed, much to Prost's fury.

The lofty viewing tower at the Circuit of the Americas affords this colourful view of Lewis Hamilton's Mercedes.

KNOW THE TRACKS 2015

Mexico returns to the Formula One calendar for 2015 as the World Championship continues to evolve. This will boost F1's Latin flavour to counter the increasingly eastward move of recent years, something augmented last year by Russia making its debut. The teams are starting to feel the strain of extra events and, with further events due for 2016, are fighting against adding any more.

The trend over the past decade has been for the World Championship to ditch its long-standing grands prix in Europe and to replace them with new and additional ones in the Middle East and Asia as part of its global expansion plan. Brand new circuits have been built for these showcase grands prix. Some have been held at day, some at night – to fit in with European TV viewing slots. Some have worked and others haven't – large crowds failed to pour through the turnstile, leaving very obvious gaps in the grandstands. However, these are simply the trials and tribulations of the push to boost the overall F1 audience.

One thing for sure, though, is that the F1 personnel have spent more time on aeroplanes than ever before as the long-time standard of 16 grands prix per year has swelled to 21, with F1 impresario Bernie Ecclestone pushing for 22 by 2016. A much-mooted and once-postponed race in New Jersey apparently no longer waits in the wings. The promoter Leo Hindery doesn't appear to have clinched the funds required for this temporary facility, meaning that F1's longstanding dream of taking a bite out of the Big Apple looks to be as far away as ever from being achieved. However, the first ever grand prix for oil-rich and image-hungry Azerbaijan, on a street circuit in capital city Baku, has been pencilled in for next year. This certainly is a place with minimal motor sport history, save for a couple of races for GT cars around its streets, so it might be best not to erect too many grandstands, but it's safe to say that, with F1, nothing ever stands still.

The Korean GP looks to be an event firmly in F1's past, despite its fleeting return in 2013. A Korean GP was listed again for 2015, but no one wants to go back to Yeongam, neither teams nor fans. It was also considered unlikely that a street race could be arranged in capital Seoul in time for its spring date, its nomination was seen merely as a stalking horse and the date was duly dropped by the FIA this January.

There had also been talk of the Indian GP after the event at Buddh International was dropped for a year, but this came to nothing, perhaps because the hassle that spoiled the teams' operations in India in the past has yet to be smoothed over to allow them to get on with their jobs.

The European season that runs from the Spanish GP in May to the Italian GP in September, interrupted only by a sidetrip to the Canadian GP in June, will run to its traditional pattern as before, save for the German GP breaking its pattern of alternation and so returning to Hockenheim rather than going to the Nürburgring. Austria's mountainside Red Bull Ring will be back for more in 2015, having entertained F1 lovers with its return race last year, its spectacular backdrop offering something very different from some of its less scenic rivals. To the east, and later in the year, Russia's second grand prix will again be held at Sochi on the temporary circuit built last year on the site that contained the headquarters when the city hosted the Olympic Winter Games in 2014. This proved to be a success when it made its F1 bow last October, its great facilities making up for a track that offers little in the way of race action.

Back for 2015, for definite, is the Mexican GP, a race last held in 1992. It will be held as before at Mexico City's Autodromo Hermanos Rodriguez, albeit with brand new pit buildings in place of the old, tatty ones and – of more importance to the drivers – the bypassing of the fearsome final corner, the Peraltada. Instead of sweeping through this long, lightly-banked righthander, they will reach the start/finish straight via a loop through the baseball stadium on the infield. What is sure to remain, though, is the passionate support of the fans as they scream out their backing for Sergio Perez. Paired with the Brazilian GP, the Mexican GP is sure to help build the end of season drama before the final round in Abu Dhabi. Fortunately, the double points allocation for the final round trialled last year will not be repeated.

This downtown venue has long hosted the season's opening round and remains a popular circuit because it's packed full of people revelling in the optimism presented by a new season.

For all of its world-beating prowess across the sporting spectrum, and despite the title-winning successes of Jack Brabham and Alan Jones, Australia's grand prix became part of the World Championship only in 1985, no doubt held back by its distance from the sport's European heartland.

When Australia joined the championship, the race went not to Sydney nor sporting capital Melbourne, but to Adelaide and its park/street circuit was an instant success.

Melbourne's F1 ambitions were not to be denied, though, and it landed the race from 1996. The venue selected was Albert Park, an urban zone located a mile south of the city's business district. The park had hosted motor races, including the non-championship Australian GP, in the 1950s, but that didn't deter protesters who were set against it. However, the race organizers agreed to invest heavily in the park's facilities for year-round use and so a circuit was laid out around its lake.

Typically, this sports-mad city embraced the race from the outset, with grandstands and hospitality areas filled on all three days of the meeting. Backed up by a packed programme of supporting races, the grand prix offers more entertainment throughout race day than any other.

Damon Hill was gifted victory in 1996, when an oil leak cost his Williams team-mate Jacques Villeneuve victory on his debut. Hill then won again in 1997, but the 1998 race was more memorable because David Coulthard surprised onlookers by letting McLaren team-mate Mika Hakkinen through to win in order to honour a pre-race agreement. Michael Schumacher scored a hat-trick of wins from 2000 to 2002.

68

INSIDE TRACK
AUSTRALIAN GRAND PRIX

Date:	**15 March**
Circuit name:	**Albert Park**
Circuit length:	**3.295 miles/5.300km**
Number of laps:	**58**
Email:	**enquiries@grandprix.com.au**
Website:	**www.grandprix.com.au**

PREVIOUS WINNERS	
2005	**Giancarlo Fisichella** RENAULT
2006	**Fernando Alonso** RENAULT
2007	**Kimi Raikkonen** FERRARI
2008	**Lewis Hamilton** McLAREN
2009	**Jenson Button** BRAWN
2010	**Jenson Button** McLAREN
2011	**Sebastian Vettel** RED BULL
2012	**Jenson Button** McLAREN
2013	**Kimi Raikkonen** LOTUS
2014	**Nico Rosberg** MERCEDES

Flow of the lap: The early part of the lap is nothing special and is brought to a near standstill at Turn 3, when the drivers have to drop to second gear for this tight right. There's then a run flanked by trees down to Turn 6 before the track opens up around the far side of the park's lake. The sequence from Turn 10 to Turn 13 is the most flowing stretch. Then it's back to a run of short bursts of power between the four 90-degree corners that complete the lap.

Best passing spot: Drivers often attempt passing moves into Turn 1 on the opening lap and try again when the field is still bunched into Turn 3. Once the field has strung out, overtaking manoeuvres at either of these corners are less likely to result in collisions and drivers often attempt passing moves into Turn 13 as well.

Fastest point: The run from Turn 10 to Turn 13 has a high average speed, but the greatest velocity is recorded at the braking point for Turn 1, at 188mph (303kph).

Most challenging corner: Fifth gear Turn 11 on the far side of the lake is the trickiest of the 16 corners on offer: the exit is blind on entry and the corner that follows arrives almost immediately after it. This makes any poor line choice costly for the drivers.

Marina
Clark
Lauda
Whiteford
Jones Chicane
Waite
Ascari
Senna
Hill
Prost
Pit Lane

Gear **1 111** *Km/h* **1** *Timing sector* ⚠ *DRS detection* 🔺 *DRS activation*

2014 POLE TIME: HAMILTON (MERCEDES),
1M44.231S, 113.809MPH/183.158KPH
2014 WINNER'S AVERAGE SPEED:
121.203MPH/195.058KPH

2014 FASTEST LAP: ROSBERG (MERCEDES),
1M32.478S, 128.273MPH/206.436KPH
LAP RECORD: M SCHUMACHER (FERRARI),
1M24.125S, 141.016MPH/226.944KPH, 2004

SEPANG

If this Malaysian beauty isn't the very best circuit of the season, then it's right up there and provides the drivers with more opportunities to overtake on each lap than any other track.

When circuit designer Hermann Tilke produced the Sepang circuit, set among the palm plantations alongside capital city Kuala Lumpur's airport in 1999, it was an instant hit. Wide and flowing, it offered a release from some of the older circuits that had begun to feel too restrictive for the cars' ever greater performance. Here, they had space to try different lines and to overtake, something that was augmented by the two long straights either side of the main grandstand and the hairpins at their ends. Helping the drivers to make their passing moves, the circuit is unusually wide on corner entry.

Of course, since the track is located in the tropics, drivers not only have to contend with soaring temperatures and sapping humidity, but the sudden arrival of savage downpours that have shaped more

than a few of Sepang's races. One example of this was in 2001, when Ferrari recovered from having both drivers spin off on oil to guess tyre choice correctly – fitting intermediates rather than rain rubber, helping Michael Schumacher to win. The rain was far heavier in 2009, when Jenson Button mastered it best to be in front when the race was stopped early and never restarted as darkness fell.

While the Malaysian GP was created to boost national prestige and to increase F1's global spread, there were no Malaysian F1 drivers for the fans to cheer until Alex Yoong stepped up in 2002. However, he was never able to score a point before he stepped down from the sport's top level and the nation's racing fans are awaiting the elevation of the next Malaysian to F1, with Jazeman Jaafar its best bet.

INSIDE TRACK
MALAYSIAN GRAND PRIX

Date:	**29 March**
Circuit name:	**Sepang Circuit**
Circuit length:	**3.444 miles/5.542km**
Number of laps:	**56**
Email:	**inquiries@sepangcircuit.com.my**
Website:	**www.malaysiangp.com.my**

PREVIOUS WINNERS	
2005	**Fernando Alonso** RENAULT
2006	**Giancarlo Fisichella** RENAULT
2007	**Fernando Alonso** McLAREN
2008	**Kimi Raikkonen** FERRARI
2009	**Jenson Button** BRAWN
2010	**Sebastian Vettel** RED BULL
2011	**Sebastian Vettel** RED BULL
2012	**Fernando Alonso** FERRARI
2013	**Sebastian Vettel** RED BULL
2014	**Lewis Hamilton** MERCEDES

Flow of the lap: This is a track that really flows and encourages a driver on without fear of constant interruptions. The blast to the first corner is wide and the righthand hairpin there is followed immediately by a lefthand hairpin, with a tight exit from the first corner required for the fastest line through the second. Unusually, the track is wide enough for various lines. Then it opens out through a long, fast righthand sweep until the uphill arrival for tight Langkawi. Fast sweepers follow down to a hairpin at Turn 9, then an arcing climb to Turn 11 before sweeping down to Sunway Lagoon before a high-speed sweeper and then a blast up the return straight.

Best passing spot: Since the advent of DRS, passing is easier at all circuits, but passing remains most likely into the first and last corners, thanks to the long straights feeding them and the generous width of track.

Fastest point: The entry to the last corner is reached at 190mph (306kph), a fraction faster than the entry to the first corner, due to the more open bend that feeds onto the straight.

Most challenging corner: The sequence of Turns 5 and 6, both taken in sixth gear, is a real test of both a driver's nerve and a car's balance, enabling extra speed to be carried down to Turn 7.

Gear **1** 111 Km/h **1** Timing sector ⚠ DRS detection ⚠ DRS activation

2014 POLE TIME: **HAMILTON (MERCEDES)**, 1M59.431S, 103.820MPH/167.082KPH

2014 WINNER'S AVERAGE SPEED: **115.228MPH/185.442KPH**

2014 FASTEST LAP: **HAMILTON (MERCEDES)**, 1M43.066S, 120.304MPH/193.611KPH

LAP RECORD: **MONTOYA (WILLIAMS)**, 1M34.223S, 131.991MPH/212.419KPH, 2004

SHANGHAI

Opened to gasps of admiration in 2004, this circuit has since become regarded as being too large because its grandstands are only part-filled, but some of the racing is excellent.

Other than racing on the street circuit in the Portuguese enclave of Macau, China had no involvement with motor racing on its mainland until the 1990s, when Zhuhai held a street race and then built a track with a view to hosting a World Championship round in 1998. This came to nothing, but six years later China entered F1 in style with its standard-setting Shanghai International Circuit.

The sheer scale of the giant pit buildings and lofty main grandstand built opposite, connected by huge, wing-like bridges, can only impress, as their like had never been seen before. However, the circuit feels like a misfit since those attending seem dwarfed by the environment. The misty weather that often cloaks the circuit in the spring only adds to this feeling.

Built to the north of bustling Shanghai,

the circuit is a miracle of engineering: it rises from marshy land that was made stable enough to build on by the sinking of thousands of 46ft/14m-deep polystyrene blocks into the ground and the use of 40,000 concrete piles.

Designed by Hermann Tilke, the circuit is in the shape of the Shang symbol, with a mixture of every type of corner around its 3.390 mile (5.450km) lap, including one of F1's longest straights between Turns 13 and 14.

The 2007 Chinese GP remains the most exciting held here because Lewis Hamilton, mastering changing conditions, looked set not only for victory but the drivers' title as well. Then he slid off into a gravel trap when pitting for dry tyres, handing victory to Ferrari's eventual champion, Kimi Raikkonen.

INSIDE TRACK
CHINESE GRAND PRIX

Date:	12 April
Circuit name:	Shanghai International Circuit
Circuit length:	3.390 miles/5.450km
Number of laps:	56
Email:	f1@china-sss.com
Website:	www.f1china.com.cn

PREVIOUS WINNERS	
2005	**Fernando Alonso** RENAULT
2006	**Michael Schumacher** FERRARI
2007	**Kimi Raikkonen** FERRARI
2008	**Lewis Hamilton** McLAREN
2009	**Sebastian Vettel** RED BULL
2010	**Jenson Button** McLAREN
2011	**Lewis Hamilton** McLAREN
2012	**Nico Rosberg** MERCEDES
2013	**Fernando Alonso** FERRARI
2014	**Lewis Hamilton** MERCEDES

Flow of the lap: Turn 1 is the start of a long right that rises to Turn 2 and then drops down before switching left at Turn 3. On the level again, it's then a blast to Turn 6 before the track doubles back on itself and runs through fast and sweeping esses behind the paddock along to Turn 9. Accelerating hard through Turn 10, the drivers have to brake heavily next at Turn 11, where they run through the reverse of Turns 1–3 before hitting the back straight. This is featureless until the drivers reach the canopied grandstands that flank the hairpin at its end. The final corner is a tricky left out of which many cars run wide.

Best passing spot: The lap sports two key places that are suitable for overtaking, into Turn 1 and into Turn 14. On lap 1, though, when the cars are bunched, drivers also make moves into Turns 2, 3 and 6.

Fastest point: At the end of the long back straight, cars just hit 200mph (322kph) before having to brake extremely hard for the Turn 14 hairpin.

Most challenging corner: The sweeping left-right of Turns 7 and 8 behind the paddock are reckoned to be the part of the lap where the drivers really have to hang onto their cars the most.

Gear **1** 111 Km/h · **1** Timing sector · ⚠ DRS detection · ▲ DRS activation

2014 POLE TIME: **HAMILTON (MERCEDES),** 1M53.860S, 107.184MPH/172.497KPH
2014 WINNER'S AVERAGE SPEED: 117.335MPH/188.833KPH

2014 FASTEST LAP: **ROSBERG (MERCEDES),** 1M40.402S, 121.551MPH/195.618KPH
LAP RECORD: **M. SCHUMACHER (FERRARI),** 1M32.238S, 132.202MPH/212.759KPH, 2004

SAKHIR

It was a brave decision to send Formula One into the desert for the first time when Bahrain made its World Championship bow back in 2004, but this arid venue now feels truly established.

There had been a stab at introducing motor racing to the Middle East in the 1980s when a temporary circuit was marked out around a plot of land next to a hotel in Dubai. That was for one event only, though, and it took until 2004 for any of the Arab states to host a round of the World Championship.

With its obvious desire to host as many top sporting events as possible, it was expected that Dubai would be the venue of choice on the Arabian peninsula. However, Bahrain beat its more high-profile neighbour to it after Crown Prince Shaikh Salman bin Hamad Al Khalifa financed this all-new circuit as part of a bid to bring in more tourists.

Built in rocky desert to the south of capital Manama at Sakhir, this Hermann Tilke-penned circuit topped by a 10-storey VIP tower was designed to offer two distinct parts. The area around the pits and paddock sports heavily watered grass verges so that it can represent an oasis, while the remainder of the lap is kept natural, representing the desert. Indeed, the desert setting causes particular problems, with the rocky verges sprayed with glue to suppress the sandstorms that can spring up suddenly and leave the circuit considerably more slippery than on the lap before. With some notably quick corners on the return leg from Turn 4, this was something that caused concern among the drivers.

Michael Schumacher won the first race here, but then Fernando Alonso and Felipe Massa showed a liking for the place by winning a pair apiece. Alonso has since added a third win before Sebastian Vettel bagged a pair in 2012 and 2013.

INSIDE TRACK
BAHRAIN GRAND PRIX

Date:	19 April
Circuit name:	Bahrain International Circuit
Circuit length:	3.363 miles/5.412km
Number of laps:	57
Email:	info@bic.com.bh
Website:	www.bahraingp.com.bh

PREVIOUS WINNERS		
2005	Fernando Alonso	RENAULT
2006	Fernando Alonso	RENAULT
2007	Felipe Massa	FERRARI
2008	Felipe Massa	FERRARI
2009	Jenson Button	BRAWN
2010	Fernando Alonso	FERRARI
2012	Sebastian Vettel	RED BULL
2013	Sebastian Vettel	RED BULL
2014	Lewis Hamilton	MERCEDES

Flow of the lap: When designing the Bahrain International Circuit, Hermann Tilke followed his long-favoured approach of having a lengthy pit straight feeding into a tight first corner. This righthander is followed directly by a kinked left that bunches the cars on the opening lap. Entering the desert sector, the track stretches away to a distant hairpin at Turn 4 before doubling back down a gentle slope through a great set of sweepers before tighter Turn 8. Turn 10 then bunches the cars again before they accelerate behind the paddock down to the more open Turn 11. From here, the track continues to opens out and rises again, reaching its highest point at Turn 13, from which a long straight and a double-kinked right brings the cars back into the oasis sector and the pit straight.

Best passing spot: Most drivers fancy their chances into Turn 1 on lap 1, though it's also important to be in position for Turn 2 to blast onto the run to Turn 4, where further moves are possible.

Fastest point: The entry to Turn 1 is reached at 186mph (300kph), which is a shade faster than the maximum velocity achieved on the downhill approach to Turn 14.

Most challenging corner: Managing to hold the widest line through Turn 11 is vital to carry speed onto the serpentine ascent to Turn 13.

Gear **1** **111** Km/h **1** Timing sector ⚠ DRS detection ▲ DRS activation

2014 POLE TIME: ROSBERG (MERCEDES),
1M33.185S, 129.916MPH/209.080KPH
2014 WINNER'S AVERAGE SPEED:
115.249MPH/185.476KPH

2014 FASTEST LAP: ROSBERG (MERCEDES),
1M37.020S, 124.781MPH/200.816KPH
LAP RECORD: M SCHUMACHER (FERRARI),
1M30.252S, 134.262MPH/216.074KPH, 2004

BARCELONA

Part of the F1 calendar since 1991, this circuit to the north of Barcelona doesn't provide exciting racing and is little liked, but it's now a must-visit venue for Fernando Alonso's Spanish fans.

Spain has held grands prix since 1913 and a round of the World Championship from 1951, but it never had a driver to excite the nation until Fernando Alonso came along in the 21st century. Alfonso de Portago might have become a sporting legend to draw the nation's attention away from its first love, football, but he was killed on the Mille Miglia in 1957. The grand prix moved from Pedralbes in the streets of Barcelona to purpose-built Jarama in the late 1960s, then on to Jerez in the country's far south in the late 1980s. Only when the race came to the Circuit de Catalunya, a dozen miles north of Barcelona, in 1991, did it feel like it had reached a venue worthy of hosting a grand prix. Yet, although the likes of Nigel Mansell and Ayrton Senna starred here, there was no Spanish driver to encourage the country to give up its first choice of motorsport, motorcycle racing, in which the country's riders had been achieving notable success.

Then along came Fernando Alonso in 2001 and all that changed as he was clearly a star in the making. Once he had joined Renault in 2003, he became ready to challenge for the title and second place that year behind Michael Schumacher's Ferrari was repeated in 2005. Then in 2006 came the world title that sent his fans wild. His value to the race organizers could not have been clearer: the grandstands and spectator banks were filled like never before.

The circuit also became something of a home from home for the teams because it was their winter testing venue of choice due both to its usually clement weather and its variety of corners.

INSIDE TRACK
SPANISH GRAND PRIX

Date:	10 May
Circuit name:	Circuit de Catalunya
Circuit length:	2.892 miles/4.654km
Number of laps:	66
Telephone:	(34) 935 719700
Website:	www.circuitcat.com

PREVIOUS WINNERS		
2005	**Kimi Raikkonen** McLAREN	
2006	**Fernando Alonso** RENAULT	
2007	**Felipe Massa** FERRARI	
2008	**Kimi Raikkonen** FERRARI	
2009	**Jenson Button** BRAWN	
2010	**Mark Webber** RED BULL	
2011	**Sebastian Vettel** RED BULL	
2012	**Pastor Maldonado** WILLIAMS	
2013	**Fernando Alonso** FERRARI	
2014	**Lewis Hamilton** MERCEDES	

Flow of the lap: Built on a hillside, the Circuit de Catalunya is given its flow by changes in gradient rather than by sequences of flowing corners. The pit straight feeds down a gentle incline to the first corner, then turns right and swiftly left before a lengthy right takes the cars up a climb that combines with the 180-degree righthander that follows up to the Seat hairpin. Having turned left there, the track plunges down to Turn 6. It then levels out and runs back towards the paddock before turning sharply left and up again out of Wurth. The lap's highest point is Campsa, a corner with an exit that's blind until at the apex. Then it's downhill again to La Caixa before another climb to a third high point, the exit of Banc de Sabadell. The final section brings the cars down out of Turn 13, through a chicane and onto the pit straight.

Best passing spot: Elf is the only realistic place to overtake, after catching a tow down the pit straight. On the opening lap, though, many a move is attempted into Turn 2 as the cars scramble, many offline, for position.

Fastest point: Cars can hit 190mph (305kph) on the approach to Elf.

Most challenging corner: Campsa is the trickiest, with its position on the brow of a hill making its apex hard to spot.

2014 POLE TIME: HAMILTON (MERCEDES), 1M25.232S, 122.151MPH/196.584KPH
2014 WINNER'S AVERAGE SPEED: 113.270MPH/182.291KPH

2014 FASTEST LAP: VETTEL (RED BULL), 1M28.918S, 117.088MPH/188.435KPH
LAP RECORD: RAIKKONEN (FERRARI), 1M21.670S, 127.500MPH/205.192KPH, 2008

MONACO

There is nowhere like this mad, narrow track in Monte Carlo, and it remains by far the most identifiable World Championship venue, even to those who don't follow motor racing.

It's infinitely easier to understand why racing was held around the streets of this Mediterranean principality back in 1929, when it first took place, than it is now. After all, inaugural Monaco GP winner William Grover-Williams lapped his Bugatti T35B at an average speed of just 50mph (80kph) back then, a speed that was far more suited to the ascent from the harbour to Casino Square and then back again than current average speeds, which are close to double that.

Yet this is a venue that defies logical concerns over whether modern F1 cars are suitable for the strictures of the place by offering all the glitz and glamour that a grand prix can possibly bestow on the World Championship. Sponsors love to be seen here, to meet the celebrities and VIPs who flock to the event and to entertain clients on huge yachts in the harbour. The racing, to a certain extent, is a peripheral to the schmoozing.

Since it's almost impossible to overtake at Monaco – the track is extremely narrow and hemmed in by crash barriers – qualifying on pole position is more important here than at any other circuit visited all year. This is one of the reasons why pole king Ayrton Senna made the place his own. Indeed, had he not crashed out of a clear lead in 1988, handing the race to his McLaren team-mate Alain Prost, the Brazilian ace's win here in 1993 would have been his seventh Monaco victory. Before his domination in the principality, Graham Hill became known as 'Mr Monaco' when he won five times between 1963 and 1969, a feat equalled by Michael Schumacher when he claimed his fifth win in 2001.

Flow of the lap: Narrow, steep and seldom straight for more than a few seconds, Monaco's circuit is a challenge to drivers, not in terms of its physicality but in terms of the concentration it demands. Even the pit straight is curving. The climb from Ste Devote to Massenet is steeper than it looks. The track then drops out of Casino Square and keeps descending through two hairpins until reaching Portier. The run through the arcing tunnel is distinctive before a gentle slope down to the harbourfront chicane. Tabac is a testing corner, followed by the pair of blind esses around the swimming pool. La Rascasse is slow, with an uphill exit and Anthony Noghes spits the cars over a brow onto the pit straight again.

Best passing spot: The best place to overtake is usually the entry to the Nouvelle Chicane.

Fastest point: It's a curving run from Portier, but cars can hit 180mph (290kph) before having to drop to 40mph (64kph) for the Nouvelle Chicane.

Most challenging corner: Massenet, as the entry is all but blind and the drivers then have to be perfectly positioned for the right through Casino Square.

73

Ste. Devote · Anthony Noghes · Casino · Mirabeau · Chicane · La Rascasse · Tunnel · Portier · START

Gear · Km/h · Timing sector · DRS detection · DRS activation

2014 POLE TIME: **ROSBERG (MERCEDES), 1M15.989S, 98.304MPH/158.205KPH**
2014 WINNER'S AVERAGE SPEED: **88.736MPH/142.807KPH**

2014 FASTEST LAP: **RAIKKONEN (FERRARI), 1M18.479S, 95.185MPH/153.185KPH**
LAP RECORD: **M SCHUMACHER (FERRARI), 1M14.439S, 100.369MPH/161.528KPH, 2004**

Although its layout is hampered by the narrow island on which it is built, the Circuit Gilles Villeneuve clearly has some magic in its DNA since it provides exciting grands prix year in, year out.

Canada first hosted a round of the Formula One World Championship in 1967, at Mosport Park, located some 45 miles (72km) to the east of Toronto. The following year, it was the province of Quebec's turn, and the grand prix moved to the Mont Tremblant circuit at Ste Jovite. The race then alternated between the two until 1970 before Mont Tremblant was dropped. Both circuits were scenic and testing but too restrictive as F1 cars became ever faster, and they lacked run-off areas. This, combined with being too far upcountry to attract the huge crowds required to make the event a financial success, meant that the Canadian GP moved again in 1978, with its new home being in Montreal.

The venue chosen was a circuit laid out around the Ile de Notre Dame on the far side of the St Lawrence Seaway from the city centre, meaning that fans could arrive by public transport – and they came in tens of thousands. Also boosting crowd numbers was local hero Gilles Villeneuve, who collected a fortunate but popular maiden win after Jean-Pierre Jarier's Lotus failed. Moving the race from the autumn, when cold weather could sweep in, to the summer in time for its fifth running in 1982 brought a very different feel to the race and there's a general party atmosphere as the teams love being in such a vibrant city.

The island had been the venue for the annual EXPO global trade fair in 1967, so the site is not only dotted with distinctive pavilions but includes a lake and a second man-made rowing lake used when the city hosted the Olympics in 1968. Space is thus at a premium and leaves the lap long and thin with a hairpin at either end.

Island Hairpin

Pont de la Concorde

Droit de Casino

L'Epingle

START

Pit Lane

5 252 | **4** 200 | **7** 300 | **5** 210 | **6** 295
4 183
4 183
8
9
2 10
11
3 102
12
6 292
3 4
14
13
7 310
1
2
3 135
7 316
3 102 | **7** 300

Gear **1** 111 Km/h **1** Timing sector ⚠ DRS detection ⚠ DRS activation

---

INSIDE TRACK
CANADIAN GRAND PRIX

Date:	**7 June**
Circuit name:	**Circuit Gilles Villeneuve**
Circuit length:	**2.710 miles/4.361km**
Number of laps:	**70**
Email:	**info@circuitgillesvilleneuve.ca**
Website:	**www.circuitgillesvilleneuve.ca**

PREVIOUS WINNERS

2004	**Michael Schumacher** FERRARI
2005	**Kimi Raikkonen** McLAREN
2006	**Fernando Alonso** RENAULT
2007	**Lewis Hamilton** McLAREN
2008	**Robert Kubica** BMW SAUBER
2010	**Lewis Hamilton** McLAREN
2011	**Jenson Button** McLAREN
2012	**Lewis Hamilton** McLAREN
2013	**Sebastian Vettel** RED BULL
2014	**Daniel Ricciardo** RED BULL

Flow of the lap: The pit straight kinks to the right before feeding into a 90-degree lefthander that is almost always the scene of contact on lap 1. Then comes a wide righthand hairpin. From here, there's little space to run two abreast through the Turn 3 and Turn 4 esses and on down the wall-lined stretch of track through fast Turn 5 and slow Turn 6 to a second esse, at Turn 8. Drivers then must get into position for the approach to the Turn 10 hairpin, L'Epingle. Accelerating hard out of here, they power through a kink at Turn 11 and then down alongside the rowing lake all the way to the final corner, a tight esse onto the pit straight, with any slip-up resulting in a clash with a wall.

Best passing spot: The first two corners produce a host of passing moves, but in the remainder of the race moves tend to be made, sometimes, into L'Epingle and, more often, into the final esse.

Fastest point: The approach to Turn 13, in eighth gear, can produce speeds of a shade under 200mph (322kph).

Most challenging corner: The Turn 8 and Turn 9 esse is really hard to get right, but it is essential to do so not just for a quick lap time in qualifying but to stand a chance of passing into L'Epingle in the race.

2014 POLE TIME: **ROSBERG (MERCEDES),**
1M14.874S, 130.299MPH/209.696KPH
2014 WINNER'S AVERAGE SPEED:
114.718MPH/184.621KPH

2014 FASTEST LAP: **MASSA (WILLIAMS),**
1M18.504S, 124.274MPH/200.000KPH
LAP RECORD: **BARRICHELLO (FERRARI),**
1M13.622S, 132.511MPH/213.256KPH, 2004

RED BULL RING

This is the circuit that added a really welcome dose of beautiful scenery to the World Championship when it returned to the F1 roster in 2014, and it provided a cracking race too.

From the moment that this venue opened for racing in 1969, as the Osterreichring, it was a hit. Draped across a hillside in the Styrian region, it looked down over the flat valley floor where the Austrian GP had been held in 1964 on a temporary and uninteresting circuit laid out on the Zeltweg military airfield. With swooping corners on a track that ran up, across and then down a hill, the Osterreichring could not have been more different. The drivers loved it and the scenery couldn't have been more picture-perfect.

One of the key features of the Osterreichring was that it was packed with high-speed corners, with race-winning average speeds of more than 130mph (209kph), even after a chicane had been inserted to slow the first corner, Hella Licht, after Mark Donohue's fatal accident

there in 1975. The race was held at the Osterreichring until 1987, a year marred by three starts because of startline crashes.

Ten years on, in 1997, F1 returned to a circuit that had been shortened by a mile and was now named the A1-Ring in deference to a mobile telephone company that had financed its redevelopment. With the western end of the circuit having been removed as the track turned up the hillside sooner after the first corner, the flow of old was gone, and the key corners tightened. This changed its nature, but it was still fun. After 2003, though, with F1 becoming ever more global and European races being shed to make way for venues further afield, Austria lost out.

Until 2014 that is, when the track, now called the Red Bull Ring, was back on the World Championship roster.

Gear ⚙ 111 Km/h ❶ Timing sector

2014 POLE TIME: MASSA (WILLIAMS), 1M08.759S, 140.735MPH/226.492KPH
2014 WINNER'S AVERAGE SPEED: 130.197MPH/209.532KPH

2014 FASTEST LAP: PEREZ (FORCE INDIA), 1M12.142S, 134.138MPH/215.875KPH
LAP RECORD: M SCHUMACHER (FERRARI), 1M08.337S, 141.606MPH/227.894KPH, 2003

INSIDE TRACK
AUSTRIAN GRAND PRIX

Date:	**21 June**
Circuit name:	**Red Bull Ring**
Circuit length:	**2.688 miles/4.326km**
Number of laps:	**71**
Email: **information@projekt-spielberg.at**	
Website: **www.projekt-spielberg.at**	

PREVIOUS WINNERS	
1986	**Alain Prost** McLAREN
1987	**Nigel Mansell** WILLIAMS
1997	**Jacques Villeneuve** WILLIAMS
1998	**Mika Hakkinen** McLAREN
1999	**Eddie Irvine** FERRARI
2000	**Mika Hakkinen** McLAREN
2001	**David Coulthard** McLAREN
2002	**Michael Schumacher** FERRARI
2003	**Michael Schumacher** FERRARI
2014	**Nico Rosberg** MERCEDES

Flow of the lap: The track rises sharply from the starting grid and then turns right as the drivers crest the rise into the first corner. Then it's flat-out up the hillside, climbing all the way via a kink to a righthand hairpin, Remus. Collisions are not unknown here as drivers vie for position both into and out of the corner. There's then an undulating run across the face of the slope before a gentle descent to Schlossgold, a downhill righthand hairpin. The cars then cross the hillside again in both directions before a pair of downhill lefts that complete the lap.

Best passing spot: There is overtaking, and often contact, at the first corner on the opening lap, but the bulk of overtaking moves are made by drivers who have got a good exit from there and then towed past a rival up the hill before claiming the inside line into the second corner, Remus.

Fastest point: This is just after the uphill lefthand kink before Remus, where the fastest hit 190mph (306kph).

Most challenging corner: Turn 1 is tougher than it used to be when this was the A1-Ring, as the ability to use the generous run-off there on a banzai qualifying lap has been curtailed by the insertion of a rumble strip that can upset a car.

SILVERSTONE

Circuits have come in and out of fashion, but Silverstone has always been loved. Since hosting the inaugural World Championship event in 1950, it has been one of F1's lynchpins.

In the immediate aftermath of World War II, there were plenty of airfields looking for new uses – and thank goodness someone suggested that the one at Silverstone in Northamptonshire would be ideal for motor racing. The rest is history because the first British GP, hosted there in 1948, was a success. 2015 will be the 49th time that Silverstone has hosted a World Championship round, a number actually below that of Monza and Monaco because Aintree and Brands Hatch have also shared the UK event.

Silverstone's topography is flat, as you would expect for an airfield, and the nature of the circuit has always been one of fast, open corners, the opposite of Monaco. Indeed, nobody who was there will forget the spectacle of Keke Rosberg achieving an average speed in qualifying of over 160mph (258kph) in his Williams in 1985.

The circuit has been modified from time to time since then, largely to slow the cars' progress, with the insertion of chicanes and the tightening of corners such as Stowe. A little gradient has been added, with the track dropping into Vale. The biggest change, though, has been the recent relocation of the pit and paddock complex to sit between the Club and Abbey corners, with the start line thus being moved from its former long-standing location between Woodcote and Copse.

There are two things that grands prix at Silverstone can always rely upon. The first is a sell-out crowd, as few fans are more faithful than British ones. The second is that the weather can't be relied upon, and Silverstone's nature changes wholly when summer sunshine gives way to rain.

INSIDE TRACK
BRITISH GRAND PRIX

Date:	**5 July**
Circuit name:	**Silverstone**
Circuit length:	**3.659 miles/5.900km**
Number of laps:	**52**
Email:	**sales@silverstone-circuit.co.uk**
Website:	**www.silverstone-circuit.co.uk**

PREVIOUS WINNERS	
2005	**Juan Pablo Montoya** McLAREN
2006	**Fernando Alonso** RENAULT
2007	**Kimi Raikkonen** FERRARI
2008	**Lewis Hamilton** McLAREN
2009	**Sebastian Vettel** RED BULL
2010	**Mark Webber** RED BULL
2011	**Fernando Alonso** FERRARI
2012	**Mark Webber** RED BULL
2013	**Nico Rosberg** MERCEDES
2014	**Lewis Hamilton** MERCEDES

Flow of the lap: Abbey is now the first corner rather than Copse, but it still means that the lap starts with a fast right. Farm is quick too, but heavy braking is required for Village, where drivers jostle for position and continue to do so until they reach the Wellington Straight. Passing is possible at the end of this, into Brooklands. Luffield is a double-apex right that feeds the cars through flat-out Woodcote onto the old pit straight. Copse remains a challenge, then the drivers relish the thrill of the Becketts esses. A good exit from Chapel is required for drivers to carry speed onto the Hangar Straight. Stowe, at its end, tightens, then drivers have to brake hard for Club before accelerating as early as they dare back onto the pit straight.

Best passing spot: Village is the best place on the opening lap, when the cars are bunched, then Brooklands thereafter.

Fastest point: The approach to Stowe and turn-in point to Becketts match each other, at 188mph (303kph).

Most challenging corner: The Becketts esses, which start just after Maggotts, have the drivers turning right, left, then right again in rapid succession. Get the balance wrong in any of these and speed is squandered.

Gear **1** Km/h **1** Timing sector ⚠ DRS detection ⚠ DRS activation

2014 POLE TIME: ROSBERG (MERCEDES), 1M35.766S, 137.548MPH/221.362KPH
2014 WINNER'S AVERAGE SPEED: 77.731MPH/125.096KPH

2014 FASTEST LAP: HAMILTON (MERCEDES), 1M37.176S, 135.552MPH/218.150KPH
LAP RECORD: ALONSO (FERRARI), 1M30.874S, 145.011MPH/233.373KPH, 2011

HOCKENHEIM

When the Nürburgring couldn't afford to take up its place in the German GP's pattern of alternation, Hockenheim stepped forward to remain part of the F1 show for a second straight year.

This year could be a turning point in the balance of power between Germany's two leading circuits. Since 2007, Hockenheim and the Nürburgring have alternated in hosting the German GP, and now, with its finances less than buoyant, it was announced midway through this January that Nürburgring would not be stepping forward to take its turn to host the 2015 event. Not only does it thus deny the Nürburgring its primary fixture, but it allows Hockenheim to welcome the World Championship for a second year in a row. Indeed, if the Nürburgring doesn't find a hefty amount of new money with which to secure next year's grand prix, then it could truly be a case of over and out for F1 visiting the Eifel Forest.

This battling duo couldn't be more different. Although both are surrounded by forest, the Nürburgring is blessed with rolling terrain while Hockenheim is very much on the flat. What has remained the same, though, even in the days of Nico Rosberg and Sebastian Vettel glories, is that the crowd numbers are diminishing. With this in mind, you can understand better why neither is flush with money right now.

If this year's grand prix at Hockenheim could be a classic one, preferably with a German driver, any German driver, in the mix for victory, then perhaps this will coax the fans of old back to this much curtailed layout near Heidelberg. Any fans who haven't visited since the end of the last century will be struck about how much things have changed since the forest loop was lopped off to shorten the lap in 2002, taking with it its old defining character of flat-out blasts through the forest.

INSIDE TRACK
GERMAN GRAND PRIX

Date:	19 July
Circuit name:	Hockenheim
Circuit length:	2.842 miles/4.574km
Number of laps:	67
Email:	Info@hockenheimring.de
Website:	www.hockenheimring.de

PREVIOUS WINNERS

2001	**Ralf Schumacher**	WILLIAMS
2002	**Michael Schumacher**	FERRARI
2003	**Juan Pablo Montoya**	WILLIAMS
2004	**Michael Schumacher**	FERRARI
2005	**Fernando Alonso**	RENAULT
2006	**Michael Schumacher**	FERRARI
2008	**Lewis Hamilton**	McLAREN
2010	**Fernando Alonso**	FERRARI
2012	**Fernando Alonso**	FERRARI
2014	**Nico Rosberg**	MERCEDES

Flow of the lap: While the first corner is open in nature and is followed by a decent straight, Turn 2 reveals just how much this circuit was slowed for 2002, as it doubles back on itself. After a lefthander, the lap is marked by a long, long arcing left. Then a hairpin. From this far point, the track heads back through a twisting complex back to the bowl of the Stadium. This is more familiar ground, being not high speed but certainly high volume.

Best passing spot: Turn 2 is a likely place to overtake, under heavy braking, but into the Spitzkehre hairpin - Turn 5 - is the best of all, with drivers having to pop out of a slipstream and get into position after their long top gear blast.

Fastest point: Drivers ought to be seeing 305kph on their cockpit read-outs before they get onto the brakes as late as they dare before the Spitzkehre hairpin.

Most challenging corner: The corner that is most critical to get right is Turn 2. In itself, this 150-degree righthander isn't that difficult. However, it feeds directly into a left, and entry speed and balance is vital here so that a driver can get onto the throttle as early as possible to accelerate onto the long, flat-out straight to the Spitzkehre.

Bernie Ecclestone Kurve

Parabolica

Mobil 1

Sudkurve

Spitzkehre

Gear ⚙ 111 Km/h ① Timing sector ⚠ DRS detection ⚠ DRS activation

2014 POLE TIME: ROSBERG (MERCEDES), 1M16.540S, 133.671MPH/215.123KPH
2014 WINNER'S AVERAGE SPEED: 121.922MPH/196.215KPH

2014 FASTEST LAP: HAMILTON (MERCEDES), 1M19.908S, 128.049MPH/206.075KPH
LAP RECORD: RAIKKONEN (McLAREN), 1M14.917S, 136.567MPH/219.784KPH, 2004

This Hungarian venue usually offers plenty of summer sunshine but, sadly, not much in the way of racing – it's so narrow and twisting that it presents precious few places to overtake.

The teams love spending time in Budapest, on the banks of the River Danube, in high summer, but it's hard to find many who enjoy Hungary's top-level racing circuit, which punishes those who fail to qualify well; its narrowness makes passing all but impossible come race-day and so the racing is often less than enthralling. At least, though, it represents an unusual challenge for the teams' race tacticians.

Built in 1986 with government finance on a hillside a dozen miles north-east of the capital, the Hungaroring was viewed with considerable interest when it hosted a World Championship round. At the time, the country was still communist-run and thus largely closed to sporting activities – especially one as capitalist as F1 – enjoyed on the western side of the Iron Curtain. However, the crowd that assembled to watch Nelson Piquet win for Williams was vast and the event hasn't looked back.

The circuit, however, has always been seen as too twisty to make a top-rank F1 venue, its straights too short for the drivers to shape up for a passing move and its mixture of corners too slow to build a flow. The introduction of DRS has alleviated this a bit, making passing at least possible, as shown to such good effect in 2014's exciting grand prix when Lewis Hamilton advanced up the order from the rear of the grid and Daniel Ricciardo worked his way to the front. However, qualifying position still continues to be as vital here as it does at Monaco.

The best way to create an exciting race here is to add some rain, as shown when Jenson Button mastered wet conditions in 2006 to achieve his maiden win for Honda.

INSIDE TRACK
HUNGARIAN GRAND PRIX

Date:	**26 July**
Circuit name:	**Hungaroring**
Circuit length:	**2.722 miles/4.381km**
Number of laps:	**70**
Email:	office@hungaroring.hu
Website:	**www.hungaroring.hu**

PREVIOUS WINNERS

2005	**Kimi Raikkonen** McLAREN
2006	**Jenson Button** HONDA
2007	**Lewis Hamilton** McLAREN
2008	**Heikki Kovalainen** McLAREN
2009	**Lewis Hamilton** McLAREN
2010	**Mark Webber** RED BULL
2011	**Jenson Button** McLAREN
2012	**Lewis Hamilton** McLAREN
2013	**Lewis Hamilton** MERCEDES
2014	**Daniel Ricciardo** RED BULL

Flow of the lap: The track slopes down towards the first corner - the downhill entry makes it tricky, as does the second apex. The track starts on one side of a valley, drops through the hairpin at Turn 2 and the righthander that follows and then carries on down to the valley floor, before climbing through fast Turn 4 and then Turn 5, a tight righthander. The track then wiggles its way along a level stretch in front of the spectator banking on the far side of the valley until it reaches Turn 11. The track then drops into the valley again before starting its climb back up the opposite slope to the pit straight via the 90-degree right at Turn 12 and the two hairpins that complete the lap.

Best passing spot: The only real option at the Hungaroring is into Turn 1, with Turn 2 possible for passing only on the opening lap for cars of similar speed.

Fastest point: Peak velocity is 185mph (298kph), which is hit just before drivers have to brake and change down to second gear for Turn 1.

Most challenging corner: Getting a good exit from Turn 2 is vital if a driver is to be on the optimum line for the downhill right kink that is Turn 3 and so carry maximum speed onto the run through to Turn 5.

Gear 🔲 **111** Km/h 🔵 Timing sector ⚠ DRS detection 🔺 DRS activation

2014 POLE TIME: ROSBERG (MERCEDES), 1M22.715S, 118.469MPH/190.658KPH
2014 WINNER'S AVERAGE SPEED: 101.091MPH/162.691KPH

2014 FASTEST LAP: ROSBERG (MERCEDES), 1M25.724S, 114.311MPH/183.9662KPH
LAP RECORD: M SCHUMACHER (FERRARI), 1M19.071S, 123.828MPH/199.282KPH, 2004

SPA-FRANCORCHAMPS

Whenever a new circuit is designed, the architect ought to first visit this Belgian marvel. Shaped over and around a wooded hillside, it has a flow and majesty that no other track can match.

This absolute gem of a circuit nestles in the Ardennes forests, 30 miles (48km) south-east of Liege and just up the road from the town of Spa.

Of course, there can be no contest in the beauty stakes between a circuit built on a piece of flat land and one that was laid out on public roads over rolling, forested hills and open farmland beyond, as Spa-Francorchamps was. So this venue, which has been operating since 1924, is always going to feel special. However, its past is dotted with dark moments since its high-speed nature and often sudden arrival of rain storms led to numerous accidents that, especially on sections through the woods, had dire outcomes.

After Pedro Rodriguez achieved a race-winning average speed of a shade under 150mph (241kph) in his BRM in 1970, it was decided that the circuit was no longer safe for the sport's premier category. So, when it next hosted a grand prix, the 8.755-mile (14.090km) lap had been cut back to 4.317 miles (6.948km) by turning right at Les Combes and cutting out the stretch through the valley between Malmedy and Stavelot, with a linking section built to join the ascent back to the pits at what is now Curve Paul Frere. If that sounds like emasculation, it was, but it left a circuit that still provided more of a challenge than most others, especially when a not infrequent visitor dropped by: rain.

The list of winners reveals that it yields only to the best, with Michael Schumacher claiming his first win here before adding five more. Ayrton Senna also was a multiple winner, with Kimi Raikkonen claiming three in a row from 2004.

INSIDE TRACK
BELGIAN GRAND PRIX

Date:	23 August
Circuit name:	Spa-Francorchamps
Circuit length:	4.352 miles/7.004km
Number of laps:	44
Email:	secretariat@spa-francorchamps.be
Website:	www.spa-francorchamps.be

PREVIOUS WINNERS

2004	**Kimi Raikkonen**	McLAREN
2005	**Kimi Raikkonen**	McLAREN
2007	**Kimi Raikkonen**	FERRARI
2008	**Felipe Massa**	FERRARI
2009	**Kimi Raikkonen**	FERRARI
2010	**Lewis Hamilton**	McLAREN
2011	**Sebastian Vettel**	RED BULL
2012	**Jenson Button**	McLAREN
2013	**Sebastian Vettel**	RED BULL
2014	**Daniel Ricciardo**	RED BULL

Flow of the lap: The short, uphill blast from the grid to La Source gives nothing away about what follows, and it's only when the cars negotiate the hairpin and plunge downhill that they get a clue. Eau Rouge is a flat-out left/right sweep into a compression, with the track kicking up sharply as the cars travel up a long climb to Les Combes. This is a right/left flick at the crest of the hill, from where the track drops through the Rivage hairpin, on down through double-apex Pouhon lefthander and then through a sequence of 90-degree bends to Paul Frere. Then it's uphill through flat-out Blanchimont to the last section, the Bus Stop chicane.

Best passing spot: A good slipstream tow up the hill from Raidillon is usually rewarded with a late-braking move into Les Combes.

Fastest point: Drivers can see 195mph (315ph) and maybe even a little more just before Les Combes and also on the climb back up the hill through Blanchimont, just before the Bus Stop.

Most challenging corner: Eau Rouge used to be fearsome, but improved aerodynamics has helped the cars' passage through there. Now the hardest corner is Pouhon, where drivers need to have their cars perfectly balanced for this downhill, sixth-gear lefthander.

2014 POLE TIME: ROSBERG (MERCEDES), 2M05.591S, 124.749MPH/200.765KPH
2014 WINNER'S AVERAGE SPEED: 135.740MPH/218.453KPH

2014 FASTEST LAP: ROSBERG (MERCEDES), 1M50.511S, 141.722MPH/228.080KPH
LAP RECORD: VETTEL (RED BULL), 1M47.263S 146.065MPH/235.069KPH, 2009

This historic Italian circuit is where the engineers can run minimum downforce and send their drivers out to slipstream their way to glory, because straightline speed is everything here.

Built in a park outside Monza to the north-west of Milan in 1922, Monza is approaching its centenary and it excites today every bit as much as it ever did as a temple both to speed and for all things Ferrari.

Pietro Bordino won the Italian GP for Fiat in 1922 and, while the trees have matured around the track, the Monza of today would still be recognizable to him: the bulk of the lap is little changed across the intervening decades, still filled with long straights and a smattering of fast corners. It offers lengthy periods at full throttle. What has been dropped, though, is the banking that made up half the lap, augmenting the lay-out still in use today to form a shape like a bent paperclip. The banking, used by F1 until 1961, is still visible, a decaying reminder of the past.

Pretty much everything at Monza has a link to the past, except for the trio of chicanes that were inserted in 1972 between the pit straight and what was Curva Grande, at Roggia and at Vialone. These were built to reduce speeds and to break up the multi-car slipstreaming packs that used to hunt there, all in the name of cutting speeds to improve safety.

With the passionate support of the *tifosi*, any Ferrari triumph is joyous, triggering cacophonous celebration. Ferrari wins have been enjoyed by Alberto Ascari in the 1950s, Phil Hill, John Surtees and Ludovico Scarfiotti in the 1960s, Clay Regazzoni and Jody Scheckter in the 1970s, Gerhard Berger in the 1980s and Michael Schumacher in the 1990s and 2000s, with Rubens Barrichello also triumphant in the 2000s. Fernando Alonso was the most recent subject of the crowd's adulation, in 2010.

INSIDE TRACK
ITALIAN GRAND PRIX

Date:	**6 September**
Circuit name:	**Autodromo Monza**
Circuit length:	**3.600 miles/5.793km**
Number of laps:	**53**
Email:	**infoautodromo@monzanet.it**
Website:	**www.monzanet.it**

PREVIOUS WINNERS

2005	**Juan Pablo Montoya** McLAREN
2006	**Michael Schumacher** FERRARI
2007	**Fernando Alonso** McLAREN
2008	**Sebastian Vettel** TORO ROSSO
2009	**Rubens Barrichello** BRAWN
2010	**Fernando Alonso** FERRARI
2011	**Sebastian Vettel** RED BULL
2012	**Lewis Hamilton** McLAREN
2013	**Sebastian Vettel** RED BULL
2014	**Lewis Hamilton** MERCEDES

Flow of the lap: The pit straight is broad, then narrows and twists sharply right and then left just beyond the old banking for the first chicane. The long right that follows, Curva Biassono, is taken in sixth gear and, just as the drivers reach the shade of the trees, they have to brake hard and jink left, then right for the second chicane. The pair of rights called Lesmo are not alike, with the second being more open, then there's a kinked straight that dips under the old, banked circuit before it reaches the third chicane. Out of Ascari, it's then flat-out behind the paddock to the final corner, from which every bit of speed at the exit helps for the blast past the pits.

Best passing spot: Any of the three chicanes offer passing opportunities, as does the entry to Curva Parabolica.

Fastest point: With wings laid back low, 212mph (341kph) can be seen at the end of the pit straight just before the first chicane, this being a fraction faster than the speed seen approaching Curva Parabolica.

Most challenging corner: Carrying enough speed through Curva Parabolica is the most testing task, and any driver running wide has to come off the power, affecting both the lap they're on and the next one.

Curva di Lesmo · Roggia · Curva Biassono · Varianye del Rettifilo · Variante Ascari · Rettifilo Tribune · Pit Lane · Curva Parabolica

Gear — Km/h · Timing sector · DRS detection · DRS activation

2014 POLE TIME: **HAMILTON (MERCEDES), 1M24.109S, 154.068MPH/247.949KPH**	2014 FASTEST LAP: **HAMILTON (MERCEDES), 1M28.004S, 147.249MPH/236.975KPH**
2014 WINNER'S AVERAGE SPEED: **144.437MPH/232.449KPH**	LAP RECORD: **BARRICHELLO (FERRARI), 1M21.046S, 159.909MPH/257.349KPH, 2004**

MARINA BAY

This is a street circuit that offers a very different challenge to the confines of Monaco because it has straights and even a few fast corners, as well as the challenge of racing after nightfall.

Singapore is known the world over for its slick city-centre district as well as the business-like way that it operates, so it came as no surprise that its desire to host a grand prix was seen through in an exemplary manner.

It's no small task to create a temporary circuit in the heart of a busy city, as closed roads can cause considerable disruption and are thus hugely unpopular. Yet Singapore's planning has worked a treat from the outset because normal life can be seen carrying on in the background even as the race is underway, with traffic motoring along on roads alongside and even over the Marina Bay circuit, despite it being right in the heart of the downtown area and including iconic buildings like City Hall, the Supreme Court and the Singapore Flyer Ferris Wheel.

Temperatures can be very high when the grand prix comes to town, and this is made worse by soaring humidity, but that isn't why the race is held at night. No, it's held at night so that its start time equates to afternoon viewing time for the key European TV market. With 1,500 lights installed, drivers can see almost as well as in daylight.

Since opening in 2008, the racing has been studded with incidents, including Felipe Massa driving off with the fuel hose still in his car in 2008 and Michael Schumacher slamming into Jean-Eric Vergne in 2012. However, its most famous race was the first one, when Fernando Alonso won for Renault, with a little too much assistance from team-mate Nelson Piquet Jr, whose deliberate spin brought out the safety car.

INSIDE TRACK
SINGAPORE GRAND PRIX

Date:	**20 September**
Circuit name:	**Marina Bay Circuit**
Circuit length:	**3.152 miles/5.073km**
Number of laps:	**61**
Email:	**info@singaporegp.sg**
Website:	**www.singaporegp.sg**

PREVIOUS WINNERS	
2008	**Fernando Alonso** RENAULT
2009	**Lewis Hamilton** McLAREN
2010	**Fernando Alonso** FERRARI
2011	**Sebastian Vettel** RED BULL
2012	**Sebastian Vettel** RED BULL
2013	**Sebastian Vettel** RED BULL
2014	**Lewis Hamilton** MERCEDES

Flow of the lap: The first corner is a tricky lefthander as it feeds straight into a right and that, in turn, goes directly into the tight left out of which drivers need to be hard on the power for the run down to Turn 5. From this righthander, drivers hit Raffles Boulevard, with a kink midway along. Then comes a sequence of three 90-degree bends and a short straight past the Singapore Cricket Club. Then there's a tricky esse after the Singapore Sling, a run across the picturesque Anderson Bridge and a hairpin left onto the second longest straight. A tight right turns the cars onto a stretch that includes six near 90-degee bends that duck under a grandstand before drivers jink left twice before arriving at the start of the pit straight.

Best passing spot: Into Turn 1 is good but that makes getting onto the right line to negotiate Turns 2 and 3 difficult. Into Turn 7 is the other main passing point.

Fastest point: Drivers can hit 185mph (298kph) - not bad for a street circuit - before they hit the brakes for Turn 7.

Most challenging corner: On lap 1, getting the first three turns strung together without hitting a rival or being hit by a rival is hard, and it's harder still to emerge onto the following straight having gained a few places. After that, carrying as much speed as possible through Turns 20 and 21 is critical for good speed back to Turn 1.

Gear 🔧 *111* Km/h ● *Timing sector* ⚠ *DRS detection* 🔺 *DRS activation*

2014 POLE TIME: **HAMILTON (MERCEDES), 1M45.681S, 107.210MPH/172.538KPH**
2014 WINNER'S AVERAGE SPEED: **94.316MPH/151.787KPH**

2014 FASTEST LAP: **HAMILTON (MERCEDES), 1M50.417S, 102.611MPH/165.137KPH**
LAP RECORD: **RAIKKONEN (FERRARI), 1M45.599S, 107.358MPH/172.776KPH, 2008**

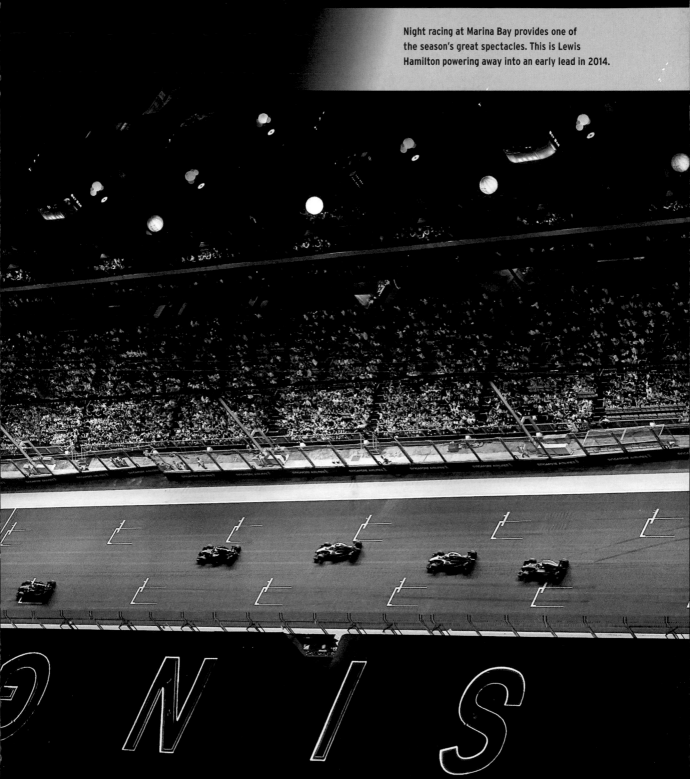

Night racing at Marina Bay provides one of the season's great spectacles. This is Lewis Hamilton powering away into an early lead in 2014.

SUZUKA

Both rain and wind have affected grands prix at Suzuka in the past, but the track is more than enough of a challenge even in the dry and no victory here comes without a supreme effort.

Despite the sudden growth in the 1960s of Japan's automotive industry, it took until 1976 for Japan to host a grand prix, at Fuji Speedway. However, this proved to be shortlived because it was dropped from the World Championship after a marshal and a spectator were killed in 1977. Incredibly, Japan dropped off F1's radar for 10 years. When it returned, in 1987, the race was hosted at another circuit, Suzuka, located 90 miles (145km) east of Osaka.

Sited on a sloping piece of land in a funfair complex from which you can see the coast, this was a circuit that had been built as long ago as 1962, originally as a test facility for Honda. As a consequence of this test brief, designer John Hugenholtz included almost every type of corner, which is why it's such a challenge.

When the F1 teams saw it for the first time, Gerhard Berger came out on top for Ferrari. Since then, races at Suzuka have never failed to entertain, often with the added thrill of its grand prix being the last of the season, with title shoot-outs between Ayrton Senna and Alain Prost in 1989 and 1990 becoming far too aggressive. In 1994, Damon Hill drove perhaps the race of his life for Williams to keep the title battle against Michael Schumacher going to the final round in Australia.

Schumacher was in the thick of things again in 1998, but stalling at the start helped Mika Hakkinen become champion for McLaren. The best move of all, though, came in 2005, when Kimi Raikkonen drove his McLaren around the outside of Giancarlo Fisichella's Renault at Turn 1 on the final lap to complete his climb from 17th on the grid to first.

INSIDE TRACK
JAPANESE GRAND PRIX

Date:	27 September
Circuit name:	Suzuka Circuit
Circuit length:	3.608 miles/5.806km
Number of laps:	53
Email:	info@suzukacircuit.com.jp
Website:	www.suzukacircuit.co.jp

PREVIOUS WINNERS	
2002	**Michael Schumacher** FERRARI
2003	**Rubens Barrichello** FERRARI
2004	**Michael Schumacher** FERRARI
2005	**Kimi Raikkonen** McLAREN
2006	**Fernando Alonso** RENAULT
2009	**Sebastian Vettel** RED BULL
2010	**Sebastian Vettel** RED BULL
2011	**Jenson Button** McLAREN
2012	**Sebastian Vettel** RED BULL
2013	**Sebastian Vettel** RED BULL
2014	**Lewis Hamilton** MERCEDES

Flow of the lap: The run to Turn 1 is gently downhill. From Turn 2, the track climbs up the slope again, with the incline increasing as it hits the esses before flattening beyond the Dunlop Curve. After Degner 1 and the tighter Degner 2, the track goes under a bridge that carries the return leg. Rounding a righthand kink, the drivers see the hairpin and have to both brake hard and get into position as they turn left to get the power down for the long right that takes them up a gentle slope to Spoon Curve. Accelerating out of this, they then have a long blast, crossing over the bridge and turning left in seventh gear at 130R. The Casio Triangle is an abrupt right/left chicane with a sharply dropping exit, then it's downhill out of the final corner past the pits to Turn 1.

Best passing spot: Turn 1 and the hairpin are the best spots for overtaking, although many attempt it into the Casio Triangle, often with unfortunate consequences.

Fastest point: The highest speed attained isn't just before Turn 1, but intead through 130R, at 190mph (306kph).

Most challenging corner: Without a doubt, getting the correct line through the four-part S-Curves is hardest of all.

Spoon Curve · Hairpin · Casino Triangle · Degner Curve · Dunlop "S" Curves · First Curve · Pit Lane

Gear **1** 111 Km/h · **1** Timing sector · ⚠ DRS detection · ⚠ DRS activation

5 230 · 6 295 · 2 70 · 2 95 · 6 260 · 7 300 · 4 185 · 7 305 · 6 260 · 5 210 · 6 285 · 5 210 · 3 140 · 5 240 · 4 160

2014 POLE TIME: ROSBERG (MERCEDES), 1M32.506S, 140.422MPH/225.987KPH
2014 WINNER'S AVERAGE SPEED. 85.167MPH/137.064KPH

2014 FASTEST LAP: HAMILTON (MERCEDES), 1M51.600S, 116.396MPH/187.322KPH
LAP RECORD: RAIKKONEN (McLAREN), 1M31.540S, 141.904MPH/228.373KPH, 2005

SOCHI

Sochi Autodrom's inaugural grand prix was held under the shadow of Russia's incursion into Ukraine, but this facility with a stunning setting looks set to remain a key part of the F1 show.

Built right in the heart of Sochi, the city on the shores of the Black Sea that hosted the Olympic Winter Games in 2014, this tailor-made circuit is very much part of the new face of the World Championship. One change for 2015, though, is that the organizers want to run the race after nightfall.

Although motor racing has been growing in Russia over the past couple of decades, it might surprise some to know that there was a Russian GP before 2014. A century before, to be precise, with the first held in 1913 and the second the following year.

Yet, after several faltering attempts to build a circuit near capital Moscow to lure the World Championship to this giant country, nothing happened until President Putin was convinced that government expenditure on hosting the Winter Olympics could be offset by using some of the facilities and infrastructure for a second event. Indeed, there are plans for the football World Cup to come here in 2018.

Benefitting from being located on the same latitude as the French Riviera, at the southernmost point of Russia, the climate is benign even in autumn and Sochi was built up as a spa town, home to sanatoria and also to Stalin's holiday home. Today, it's a playground for Russians escaping harsher climes.

The site chosen for the Sochi Autodrom contains many of the stadia built for the Winter Olympic Games, and the circuit snakes around these. It's a circuit on which drivers are able to top 200mph (320kph).

Whether the race will bring Russian fans in to the sport remains to be seen because it's a learning process for many. If Russian racer Daniil Kvyat continues his ascent, he could be the key.

INSIDE TRACK
RUSSIAN GRAND PRIX

Date:	**11 October**
Circuit name:	**Sochi Autodrom**
Circuit length:	**3.634 miles/5.848km**
Number of laps:	**53**
Email:	**info@sochiautodrom.ru**
Website:	**www.sochiautodrom.ru/en**

PREVIOUS WINNER

2014	**Lewis Hamilton** MERCEDES

Flow of the lap: The start of the lap looks simple enough, as there's an easy right kink just after the startline and then a straight. After that, going anticlockwise around one of the many Olympic stadiums, there's a tight right feeding into a really tricky semi-circular loop. Then the circuit becomes a bit of a lopsided square before opening up again out of Turn 10 at the back of the circuit onto another kinked straight down to Turn 13. The circuit then tightens up for a second time as it twists its way around behind the paddock through a series of gradient changes before drivers complete their lap with a pair of 90-degree rights.

Best passing spot: There are three main places for overtaking. The first is into Turn 2, this 90-degree righthander at the end of the start/finish straight. This was notably interesting on the opening lap in 2014 when Nico Rosberg locked up and ruined his race. The second passing place is into Turn 13, another 90-degree left. The third place is into Turn 16 – guess what, another 90-degree right.

Fastest point: The approach to Turn 2 is the fastest point on the circuit. Valtteri Bottas topped 206mph (330kph) there in his Williams in qualifying in 2014 after blasting flat-out along the kinked stretch from the final corner past the main grandstands. The approach to Turn 11 won't be far behind in the speed stakes.

Most challenging corner: Turn 3 takes this prize for being a most unusual lefthander in that it just keeps on going left, left and left some more, making life even tougher for drivers by tightening its radius as it goes.

Km/h (simulated speeds)

2014 POLE TIME: **HAMILTON (MERCEDES), 1M38.513S, 132.790MPH/213.705KPH**
2014 WINNER'S AVERAGE SPEED: **125.732MPH/202.346KPH**

2014 FASTEST LAP: **BOTTAS (WILLIAMS), 1M40.896S, 129.654MPH/208.658KPH**
LAP RECORD: **BOTTAS (WILLIAMS), 1M40.896S 129.654MPH/208.658KPH, 2014**

CIRCUIT OF THE AMERICAS

The drivers loved this undulating circuit, built near Austin, Texas, from the moment they tried it for the first time in 2012. The track's use of gradient makes racing here a real challenge.

The United States is a colossal country, measuring about 3,000 miles (4,800km) from east to west coast, from the Atlantic to the Pacific. Perhaps this is one of the reasons why its grand prix, hosted for the first time in 1959, has moved around a lot. When the all-new Circuit of the Americas hosted the United States GP for the first time in 2012, it was the ninth venue to host a grand prix in the USA.

Of course, there's always the added explanation that NASCAR stock car racing is the only sort of competition worth watching in the eyes of many of the nation's motorsport fans. Anything else is seen as too fancy and, frankly, too foreign. The constant venue changes have really taken place, though, because so few of the USA's street circuits have captured the public's imagination and long-time GP

home, Watkins Glen in New York State, had fallen behind the safety levels required for F1 racing by 1980. Even placing a grand prix in Detroit, 'Motor City', failed to impress. So, when plans were announced that the city of Austin wanted the race, people didn't expect too much.

However, the circuit was an instant hit and was clearly built to bring not just F1 but other international racing series to the USA. Furthermore, with Mexico just across the border and without a grand prix of its own until 2015, there was a clamour among Mexican fans wanting to watch their great F1 hope Sergio Perez go for glory.

The design of the circuit, set on a wonderfully rolling landscape, has a great flow to it, no doubt down to a design that includes as many great corners from other circuits as possible.

INSIDE TRACK
UNITED STATES GRAND PRIX

Date:	**25 October**
Circuit name:	**Circuit of the Americas**
Circuit length:	**3.400 miles/5.472km**
Number of laps:	**56**
Email:	**info@circuitoftheamericas.com**
Website:	**www.circuitoftheamericas.com**

PREVIOUS WINNERS		
2012	**Lewis Hamilton** McLAREN	
2013	**Sebastian Vettel** RED BULL	
2014	**Lewis Hamilton** MERCEDES	

Flow of the lap: Just like Austria's Red Bull Ring, this circuit starts its lap with a steep climb to the first corner, rising 130ft (40m) fro the startline. After levelling off, the track doubles back and plunges down to Turn 2 before levelling off again and running through a wonderful sequence of esses. On reaching Turn 11, the furthest point from the pits, drivers accelerate out of this lefthand hairpin for the appreciable back straight. This has another hairpin at its end before the drivers reach the least flowing section of the track, with tight turns through to Turn 15, then a long righthander between Turns 16 and 18. The lap is completed by a slow final corner – drivers must then get the power down as soon as they dare in order to carry as much speed as possible up the pit straight and then up the hill to Turn 1.

Best passing spot: In 2013, Mark Webber proved that Turn 12 can be the spot when he lined up Lewis Hamilton's Mercedes into this lefthand hairpin and passed it with a masterful piece of late braking. A year later, Hamilton did the same there to team-mate Nico Rosberg. Also, on lap 1, Turn 1 is also the scene of many passing moves.

Fastest point: Cars reach speeds in excess of 190mph (306kph) on the approach to Turn 12 before braking for this lefthand hairpin.

Most challenging corner: For sheer driver satisfaction, an inch-perfect run through a sequence of esses takes some beating. Think of the S-Curves at Suzuka or Becketts at Silverstone. It's the same here, with the run from Turn 3 to Turn 6.

Gear 🅚111 Km/h 🅚 Timing sector ⚠ DRS detection ⚠ DRS activation

2014 POLE TIME: **ROSBERG (MERCEDES),**
1M36.067S, 128.371MPH/206.593KPH
2014 WINNER'S AVERAGE SPEED:
114.870MPH/184.866KPH

2014 FASTEST LAP: **VETTEL (RED BULL),**
1M41.379S, 121.645MPH/195,769MPH
LAP RECORD: **VETTEL (RED BULL), 1M39.347S,**
124.132MPH/199.772KPH, 2012

MEXICO CITY

Talk that Formula One was going to return to Mexico for the first time since 1992 started in 2014. That talk is now a reality and racing will resume this November on a circuit steeped in history.

Built back in 1962 in the eastern outskirts of rapidly expanding Mexico City, the circuit was the government's response to the huge popularity on the world scene of the Mexican drivers and brothers, Pedro and, especially, Ricardo Rodriguez. Laid out around a park, the circuit was notably open and fast, feeling especially so avenues of trees lined much of its route.

The first Mexican GP, a non-championship event, was held at the end of that season and it was supposed to be a celebration of the country's new place on the sport's top table. However, it turned to tragedy when Ricardo crashed his Rob Walker Racing Lotus fatally in practice at the circuit's trickiest corner, the lightly banked Curva Peraltada, which feeds the cars back onto the start/finish straight.

Mexico duly became part of the World Championship in 1963, with Jim Clark winning, and the race continued until 1970. However, one of the worst features of the circuit was an almost complete absence of crowd control and fans scared the drivers by flooding down the grass banking that surrounded much of the circuit, standing literally at the edge of the track. In 1970, this caused the event to descend into chaos and F1 declined to return until 1986, when Gerhard Berger took his first F1 win for Benetton. After 1992, though, Mexico dropped off the calendar and was later used by CART, secondary level NASCAR and then A1GP.

Altitude has a role to play here because Mexico City's location 6,000ft (1,830m) above sea level means that engines, especially turbocharged ones, struggle with the lack of oxygen.

INSIDE TRACK
BRAZILIAN GRAND PRIX

Date:	**1 November**
Circuit name:	**Autodromo Hermanos Rodriguez**
Circuit length:	**2.747 miles/4.421km**
Number of laps:	**70**
Email:	**rosario@cie.com.mx**
Website:	
www.autodromohermanosrodriguez.com.mx	

PREVIOUS WINNERS

1968	**Graham Hill** LOTUS
1969	**Denny Hulme** McLAREN
1970	**Jacky Ickx** FERRARI
1986	**Gerhard Berger** BENETTON
1987	**Nigel Mansell** WILLIAMS
1988	**Alain Prost** McLAREN
1989	**Ayrton Senna** McLAREN
1990	**Alain Prost** FERRARI
1991	**Riccardo Patrese** WILLIAMS
1992	**Nigel Mansell** WILLIAMS

Flow of the lap: The main straight is long and wide, heading away from the pits flanked by tree-lined parkland. The first corner, Espiral, requires heavy braking, as it's a 90-degree right. This feeds into a left-right esse before a secondary straight takes the cars down to the Lake Esses. The furthest point from the pits is the Horquilla hairpin and the return leg from this is a series of open but twisting corners, with the esses a real treat. The run behind the rear of the paddock to the final corner, the Peraltada, is where drivers steel themselves for this flat-out and hang-on final bend.

Best passing spot: With a fast corner leading onto it and a good length, the pit straight provides a clear opportunity for slipstreaming and there's sufficient width in the braking area to try a move into the first corner.

Fastest point: Maximum speed at this wonderfully old-fashioned circuit is achieved at the braking point before Espiral, with 190mph (306kph) likely.

Most challenging corner: It's not just on reputation that the Curva Peraltada is the circuit's toughest corner, as the challenge of its long, slightly-banked and bumpy arc is still one to focus a driver's mind.

Recta Principal · Ese Moises Solana · Recta Trasera · Ese del Lago · Horquilla · Eses · Recta del Ovalo · Peraltada · Pit Lane · START

1992 POLE TIME: **MANSELL (WILLIAMS), 1M16.346S, 129.535MPH/208.466KPH**
1992 WINNER'S AVERAGE SPEED: **123.762MPH/199.176KPH**

1992 FASTEST LAP: **BERGER (MCLAREN), 1M17.711S, 127.259MPH/204.804KPH**
LAP RECORD: **MANSELL (WILLIAMS), 1M16.788S, 128.789MPH/207.266KPH, 1991**

INTERLAGOS

This Brazilian circuit enters its 75th year in 2015 and in many ways it shows its age since modernization plans are set to be realized. What won't change, though, is the passion of the fans.

You have to love Interlagos. Its 2.667-mile (4.292km) lap is packed with interesting and challenging corners. Furthermore, its fans are the most voluble of all, cheering every move by a Brazilian driver. Best of all, though, it's a circuit that has provided some of the most dramatic races in World Championship history.

Built on a hillside beyond the southern suburbs of Sao Paulo in 1940, Interlagos – which means 'between the lakes' – started life with a lap of just under five miles (8km) as it weaved between lakes on the lower slopes. In 1990, when the Brazilian GP returned here after a 10-year spell at Rio de Janeiro's Jacarepagua, this had been cut down by two miles (3km) to its current length, with the slope giving those in the grandstands opposite the pits a view of much of the lap.

The fans have been treated to fabulous racing over the years, their greatest joy coming in 1991, when Ayrton Senna finally won his home race. For sheer drama, though, nothing comes close to when home-town hero Felipe Massa won the race – and initially the title – in 2008, only to have the title snatched from him a few seconds later by Lewis Hamilton who passed Timo Glock's Toyota to finish where he needed to.

With a deal signed to keep the Brazilian GP at Interlagos until 2020, long overdue construction work is finally set to start on a new pit and paddock complex. There had been talk of this complex being moved down the slope to the less congested area before the fourth corner, Descida do Lago, but it will now be kept in its current location at the top of the slope.

INSIDE TRACK
BRAZILIAN GRAND PRIX

Date:	**15 November**
Circuit name:	**Autodromo Jose Carlos Pace Interlagos**
Circuit length:	**2.667 miles/4.292km**
Number of laps:	**71**
Email:	**info@gpbrazil.com**
Website:	**www.gpbrazil.com**

PREVIOUS WINNERS

2005	**Juan Pablo Montoya** McLAREN
2006	**Felipe Massa** FERRARI
2007	**Kimi Raikkonen** FERRARI
2008	**Felipe Massa** FERRARI
2009	**Mark Webber** RED BULL
2010	**Sebastian Vettel** RED BULL
2011	**Mark Webber** RED BULL
2012	**Jenson Button** McLAREN
2013	**Sebastian Vettel** RED BULL
2014	**Nico Rosberg** MERCEDES

Flow of the lap: This is a lap that flows from the moment that the drivers negotiate the first corner and plunge into dipping Senna S. Out of this compression, they turn left and carry on down the slope to Descida do Lago. The track then climbs to Ferradura before running to Laranja and diving down the slope again, to Pineirinho. Then it's up once more to Cotovelo and down once again, through Mergulho to Juncao. Out of this third-gear left, drivers are then hard on the power through the long uphill arc to the pit straight and then on to the first corner.

Best passing spot: Into Turn 1, Descida do Sol, is always popular, with its long approach, but down the hill into Descida do Lago is another good spot for overtaking.

Fastest point: The fastest speed recorded is at the braking point into Turn 1, at around 197mph (317kph). This is just a few miles per hour faster than that achieved into the braking zone before Descida do Lago.

Most challenging corner: Because its entry is all but blind over a slight brow and then drops away sharply and changes camber, Descida do Sol is the toughest of all, especially if a driver is under attack and having to defend his position.

Senna "S"

Subida dos Boxes

Pit Lane

Descida do Lago

Juncao

Curva do Sol

Reta Oposta

Gear 🔧 111 Km/h 🏁 Timing sector ⚠ DRS detection 🔺 DRS activation

2014 POLE TIME: ROSBERG (MERCEDES), 1M10.023S, 137.653MPH/221.532KPH
2014 WINNER'S AVERAGE SPEED: 126.662MPH/203.843KPH

2014 FASTEST LAP: HAMILTON (MERCEDES), 1M13.555S, 131.044MPH/210.895KPH
LAP RECORD: MONTOYA (WILLIAMS), 1M11.473S, 134.837MPH/217.000KPH, 2004

YAS MARINA

This circuit was built with a money-no-object approach and its spectacular buildings add some glamour to an entertainment complex that was once a patch of scrubby desert.

When Abu Dhabi decided that Dubai was claiming all the limelight for hosting the best sporting events in the Gulf, the senior partner in the United Arab Emirates trumped Dubai's best efforts with a tourism attraction of its own. The result was the grandiose Yas Marina circuit built in a complex that includes a marina, a Ferrari theme park with a 70m (229ft) high tower, a golf course and several top-end hotels, one of which is draped over the track and provides a dramatic feature as dusk, then finally full darkness, falls over the race. These images truly stand out from the shadow of nearby Bahrain, which hosts its own grand prix each spring.

Built in 2008 on Yas Island to the east of the capital, the circuit was designed by Hermann Tilke and his clear aim was to build a track that would entertain with overtaking aplenty, as shown by the inclusion of two long straights into tight corners, offering the opportunity for late braking moves. Sadly, the reality hasn't been as spectacular as had been hoped for, with races being quite processional until DRS and KERS were introduced. Another factor that Tilke introduced was placing a chicane and hairpin – Turns 5 to 7 – right in front of a grandstand, putting the fans extremely close to the action and doing the same with the chicanes at Turns 8 and 9, then again at Turns 11 and 12.

The best race in the event's six-year history was the second one, in 2010, when Red Bull Racing's Sebastian Vettel triumphed to vault from third in the points table at this final round to first, as his chief rival Fernando Alonso's Ferrari got stuck behind Vitaly Petrov's Renault.

89

INSIDE TRACK
ABU DHABI GRAND PRIX

Date:	**29 November**
Circuit name:	**Yas Marina Circuit**
Circuit length:	**3.451 miles/5.554km**
Number of laps:	**56**
Email:	
customerservice@yasmarinacircuit.com	
Website:	**www.yasmarinacircuit.com**

PREVIOUS WINNERS	
2009	**Sebastian Vettel** RED BULL
2010	**Sebastian Vettel** RED BULL
2011	**Lewis Hamilton** McLAREN
2012	**Kimi Raikkonen** LOTUS
2013	**Sebastian Vettel** RED BULL
2014	**Lewis Hamilton** MERCEDES

Flow of the lap: The run to the first corner is enclosed by grandstands, then there's a 90-degree left that takes the cars away through an open bend, then right to the first chicane. Out of the hairpin, there's a long straight to Turn 8 and another chicane. Then, after an arcing curve, there's a straight into a third chicane. The nature of the lap then changes as the track runs around the marina, including its unique passage under a bridge with a spectacular walkway between two parts of the marina hotel. Two more moderately tight corners complete the lap. A notable feature is the way that the pits are exited via a tunnel that runs under the track just before Turn 1 to feed the cars back out onto the circuit from the lefthand rather than righthand side.

Best passing spot: The Turns 5 and 6 complex is where most of the action happens on the first lap, but the Turns 8 and 9 chicane at the end of the main straight tends to be the most used overtaking place for the remainder of the race.

Fastest point: At the braking point before Turn 8, the fastest cars can be travelling at a fraction under 200mph (322kph), which seems faster if the drivers look up to the grandstand sited straight ahead of them.

Most challenging corner: Braking as late as possible is key both to attacking and defending into Turn 8.

Gear **1** 111 *Km/h* **1** *Timing sector* ⚠ *DRS detection* ⚠ *DRS activation*

2014 POLE TIME: **ROSBERG (MERCEDES)**, 1M40.480S, 123.643MPH/198.984KPH
2014 WINNER'S AVERAGE SPEED: **114.942MPH/184.982KPH**

2014 FASTEST LAP: **RICCIARDO (RED BULL)**, 1M44.496S, 118.894MPH/191.342KPH
LAP RECORD: **VETTEL (RED BULL)**, 1M40.279S, 131.367MPH/211.463KPH, 2009

REVIEW OF THE 2014 SEASON

With a comprehensive change to the technical regulations, it was always possible that there might be a change to the established order, but few would have predicted Red Bull Racing being toppled and then dominated by Mercedes. So good was its car that Lewis Hamilton and Nico Rosberg were left to spend the year fighting only with each other.

The key to success in the radical new form of Formula One was a long lead time, and this is one of the reasons why Mercedes, and anyone driving a car powered by a Mercedes engine, did so well, leaving their Renault- and Ferrari-engined rivals feeling short of grunt.

The key change was the replacement of 2.4-litre V8s with 1.6-litre turbocharged V6 engines. These were also required to produce some of their power through energy recovery systems, giving them clear applicability to the automotive industry as it develops hybrid systems. On top of that, the teams had to accommodate a lower nose, a narrower front wing and the elimination of exhaust-blown downforce. The drivers also had to learn how and when to harness the extra power from the hybrid systems, while the different characteristics required for slowing down for corners left some finding the new cars tricky to drive.

Going into the opening race in Australia, most teams felt woefully short on running and most worried that they wouldn't achieve the race distance without running short of fuel. Yet they all exceeded their expectations. Mercedes won that race, through Nico Rosberg, but then it dawned on F1 fans that Red Bull Racing - champion constructor four years in a row - had no answer to the pace of the Silver Arrows. Its Renault engine was not up to the challenge despite Adrian Newey's typically aerodynamically excellent RB10.

When Mercedes waltzed away to a dominant one-two finish at Sepang, this time with Lewis Hamilton leading Rosberg home, the writing was clearly on the wall. When Hamilton added the next three wins to his tally, with Rosberg second in each of them, the other 10 teams would have had good cause to panic because they had nothing up their sleeves with which to boost their challenges. McLaren, despite having Mercedes engines, was nowhere and, at this stage, being shown a clean pair of heels by Force India's Mercedes-powered VJM07s, with Sergio Perez collecting third in Bahrain and Nico Hulkenberg gathering points at every round. Ferrari was also, despite Fernando Alonso's best efforts, falling short.

Perhaps the biggest shock of all, though, was that Sebastian Vettel had been knocked off his perch, not only by Mercedes' speed but from within as well. Daniel Ricciardo - promoted from Red Bull's junior team, Toro Rosso - had not only got the better of him in Australia but at almost every subsequent round. The Australian then went on to be the first driver to break Mercedes' victory run. This came in Canada when the Silver Arrows both lost their hybrid power. Still, when he went on to win an exciting Hungarian GP and then again at Spa-Francorchamps, it showed that the sport had a new star.

By mid-season, another team had risen towards the top: Williams. This was the result of an aerodynamically sleek car working effectively in the hands of Valtteri Bottas and, increasingly, Ferrari refugee Felipe Massa. Bottas claimed his first podium finish on F1's return to Austria and then backed it up with three more in the next four races. Massa took until the Italian GP to join the Mercedes drivers on a podium.

Red Bull Racing dragged itself up the rankings and ended the year second overall, albeit without a win for Vettel. Many also delighted in longstanding Williams getting back to the sharp end as it ended the year third overall.

Alonso was so demotivated by Ferrari's form that he chose to leave the team for McLaren, in the hope that its incoming Honda engines would give him better tools than he could see Ferrari having in 2015. McLaren did improve as the year went on, with Jenson Button finishing eighth in the final standings and Kevin Magnussen back in 11th.

Force India discovered late in the year that it had taken a wrong turn aerodynamically, while Scuderia Toro Rosso picked up occasional points, with rookie Daniil Kvyat impressing and Jean-Eric Vergne once again excellent. No team was in more trouble at the opening round than Lotus, its cars scarcely having done any testing, but it made late progress. Sauber was placed better initially, but its drivers never broke into the top 10.

At the tail, Marussia scored its first points, for Jules Bianchi's ninth place at Monaco, but was otherwise nowhere. It was then hit at Suzuka by Bianchi's awful accident, and closed its doors before the US GP. Caterham also had to stay away. Although it earned its reprieve for the final round, its future is far from certain.

It was a great day for Mercedes under F1's new technical rules, but not for Lewis Hamilton, whose F1 W05's engine failed early on. That left Nico Rosberg to win at a canter, with Red Bull Racing's Daniel Ricciardo later excluded from second place.

When a raft of new technical regulations are introduced, it's almost always the case that one team will start the season in much better shape than all the others. For 2014, that team was Mercedes GP. It had made the best attempt to master the arrival of smaller, turbocharged engines, a revised aerodynamic package, an increase in the amount of energy that could be gathered and reused electrically and a fuel flow limit. Problems with the last of these scuppered the effort of the previously dominant Red Bull Racing.

Lewis Hamilton led away from pole position, but his race was over after just two laps when his V6 turbo failed. The race was all about his team-mate Rosberg after that.

Ricciardo ran without trouble to finish second, 24s down. However, he went to bed knowing that the points, though not the thrill of appearing on the podium in front of his home fans, had been taken from him. The FIA disqualified him on the grounds that his Renault engine had exceeded the maximum fuel flow limit of 100kg per hour.

Thus McLaren rookie Kevin Magnussen was promoted to second, having actually backed off in the final laps, as he had insufficient fuel to spare to continue his attack. Team-mate Jenson Button was promoted to third, but this was to prove a false dawn for McLaren.

The driver who probably should have finished second was Valtteri Bottas, but the Finn clipped the wall at Turn 10 on lap 10 and was left to mount a fightback to finish fifth behind Fernando Alonso.

What of four-time World Champion Sebastian Vettel? Well, he started only 12th after being slowed by yellow flags on his qualifying laps, and was out of the race after just three laps with engine trouble.

The team that seemed to have lost the most ground, however, was Lotus, with Romain Grosjean and Pastor Maldonado covering only a handful of laps before qualifying, then ending up slowest. They both retired with ERS failures.

Nico Rosberg prepares to power his way past pole-sitting Mercedes team-mate Lewis Hamilton.

MELBOURNE ROUND 1

DATE: 16 MARCH 2014

Laps: 57 • Distance: **187.822 miles/302.271km** • Weather: **Cloudy and mild**

Pos	Driver	Team	Result	Stops	Qualifying Time	Grid
1	**Nico Rosberg**	Mercedes	1h32m58.710s	2	1m44.595s	3
D**	**Daniel Ricciardo**	Red Bull	1h33m23.235s	2	1m45.314s	2
2	**Kevin Magnussen**	McLaren	1h33m25.487s	2	1m45.745s	4
3	**Jenson Button**	McLaren	1h33m28.737s	2	1m44.437s	10
4	**Fernando Alonso**	Ferrari	1h33m33.994s	2	1m45.819s	5
5	**Valtteri Bottas**	Williams	1h33m46.349s	2	1m48.147s	15*
6	**Nico Hulkenberg**	Force India	1h33m49.428s	2	1m46.030s	7
7	**Kimi Raikkonen**	Ferrari	1h33m56.385s	2	1m44.494s	11
8	**Jean-Eric Vergne**	Toro Rosso	1h33m59.151s	2	1m45.864s	6
9	**Daniil Kvyat**	Toro Rosso	1h34m02.295s	2	1m47.368s	8
10	**Sergio Perez**	Force India	1h34m24.626s	3	1m47.293s	16
11	**Adrian Sutil**	Sauber	56 laps	1	1m45.655s	13
12	**Esteban Gutierrez**	Sauber	56 laps	2	1m35.117s	20*
13	**Max Chilton**	Marussia	55 laps	2	1m34.293s	17
NC	**Jules Bianchi**	Marussia	49 laps	2	1m34.794s	18
R	**Romain Grosjean**	Lotus	43 laps/hybrid	1	1m36.993s	22!
R	**Pastor Maldonado**	Lotus	29 laps/hybrid	1	no time	21
R	**Marcus Ericsson**	Caterham	27 laps/oil pressure	1	1m35.157s	19
R	**Sebastian Vettel**	Red Bull	3 laps/engine	0	1m44.668s	12
R	**Lewis Hamilton**	Mercedes	2 laps/engine	0	1m44.231s	1
R	**Felipe Massa**	Williams	0 laps/accident	0	1m48.079s	9
R	**Kamui Kobayashi**	Caterham	0 laps/accident	0	1m45.867s	14

FASTEST LAP: ROSBERG, 1M32.478S, 128.273MPH/206.436KPH ON LAP 19 • RACE LEADERS: ROSBERG 1–57
* 5-PLACE GRID PENALTY FOR GEARBOX CHANGE. • ! PUT TO BACK OF GRID FOR CAR BEING MODIFIED UNDER PARC FERME CONDITIONS.
** EXCLUDED FOR EXCEEDING MAXIMUM FUEL FLOW OF 100KG PER HOUR

Thwarted at the Australian GP, this was Lewis Hamilton's chance to bounce back and he took it with both hands, laying down a challenge to his Mercedes team-mate Nico Rosberg by beating him easily, while Red Bull's Sebastian Vettel found improved form to complete the podium.

After his Melbourne retirement, Lewis Hamilton experienced the challenge of making his fuel and tyres last through a grand prix governed by new regulations, and discovered how best to harness and reuse the energy through both KERS and ERS. He did it extremely well, beating Rosberg by 17s.

In fact, Rosberg's focus was more on fellow German Vettel from the start when he felt that the Red Bull Racing driver had pushed him towards the pitwall. He resisted the challenge then, at Turn 3, got sideways, allowing Hamilton to make his escape.

There was contact on lap 2, though, as Kevin Magnussen clipped Kimi Raikkonen's seventh-placed Ferrari at Turn 1, with the subsequent puncture leaving the Finn out of the points. With a damaged front wing plus a 5s stop-go penalty, the Dane dropped to ninth overall.

Over the course of the race, Rosberg simply didn't have any answers to Hamilton's pace. He would have been demoralized by the chequered flag because it was already clear that the title race was going to be between just him and his British team-mate, such was the dominance of the Mercedes team.

Fernando Alonso proved to be the best of the rest for Ferrari, getting the better of Force India's Nico Hulkenberg to take fourth.

There was an interesting development in the Williams camp as Felipe Massa ignored Williams team orders to let Valtteri Bottas past, albeit only in a fight over seventh place, in the wake of Jenson Button's McLaren.

Daniel Ricciardo might have raced to fourth place but for a blunder during his final pitstop when he was sent on his way with his front left wheel not properly attached. His car had to be pulled back to his pit to have the wheel refitted and the delay cost him 1m25s. With subsequent nose pillar damage plus a 10s penalty, he retired.

Lotus racer Romain Grosjean made a vast improvement on his Melbourne outing, and he finished just out of the points in 11th.

SEPANG ROUND 2

DATE: 30 MARCH 2014

Laps: 56 • Distance: **192.888 miles/310.424km** • Weather: **Dry and bright**

Pos	Driver	Team	Result	Stops	Qualifying Time	Grid
1	**Lewis Hamilton**	Mercedes	1h40m25.974s	3	1m59.431s	1
2	**Nico Rosberg**	Mercedes	1h40m43.287s	3	2m00.050s	3
3	**Sebastian Vettel**	Red Bull	1h40m50.508s	3	1m59.486s	2
4	**Fernando Alonso**	Ferrari	1h41m01.966s	3	2m00.175s	4
5	**Nico Hulkenberg**	Force India	1h41m13.173s	2	2m01.712s	7
6	**Jenson Button**	McLaren	1h41m49.665s	3	2m04.053s	10
7	**Felipe Massa**	Williams	1h41m51.050s	3	2m02.460s	13
8	**Valtteri Bottas**	Williams	1h41m51.511s	3	2m02.756s	18*
9	**Kevin Magnussen**	McLaren	55 laps	3	2m02.213s	8
10	**Daniil Kvyat**	Toro Rosso	55 laps	3	2m02.351s	11
11	**Romain Grosjean**	Lotus	55 laps	3	2m02.885s	15
12	**Kimi Raikkonen**	Ferrari	55 laps	3	2m01.218s	6
13	**Kamui Kobayashi**	Caterham	55 laps	2	2m03.595s	20
14	**Marcus Ericsson**	Caterham	54 laps	3	2m04.407s	22
15	**Max Chilton**	Marussia	54 laps	3	2m04.388s	21
R	**Daniel Ricciardo**	Red Bull	49 laps/front wing	5	2m00.541s	5
R	**Esteban Gutierrez**	Sauber	35 laps/gearbox	2	2m02.369s	12
R	**Adrian Sutil**	Sauber	32 laps/power unit	2	2m02.131s	17
R	**Jean-Eric Vergne**	Toro Rosso	18 laps/turbocharger	2	2m03.078s	9
R	**Jules Bianchi**	Marussia	8 laps/crash damage	1	2m02.702s	19
R	**Pastor Maldonado**	Lotus	7 laps/power unit	0	2m02.074s	16
NS	**Sergio Perez**	Force India	0 laps/gearbox	0	2m02.511s	14

FASTEST LAP: HAMILTON, 1M43.066S, 120.310MPH/193.621KPH ON LAP 53 • RACE LEADERS: HAMILTON 1–56
* 3-PLACE GRID PENALTY FOR IMPEDING DURING QUALIFYING

Delight on the podium after Hamilton and Rosberg gave Mercedes its first one-two since 1955.

BAHRAIN GP

Lewis Hamilton made it two wins in a row over Mercedes team-mate Nico Rosberg, but this one was much closer because Hamilton only just held on. Some way back, Sergio Perez gave Force India its first podium since 2009, chased by Daniel Ricciardo.

Bahrain's first grand prix to be run after nightfall was an enthralling spectacle to witness as Hamilton and Rosberg raced each other, wheel to wheel. Starting from pole, Rosberg was passed by Hamilton in the drag race down to the first corner. They then stayed close, with Hamilton's advantage just half a second when he pitted to change to soft compound tyres on lap 19.

Anxious to find an advantage, Rosberg stayed out two laps longer, then fitted mediums. He was saving his softs for the third and final stint when Hamilton would be on mediums. However, his speed advantage in the closing laps was negated by Hamilton driving a strong defensive race all the way to the chequered flag, crossing the line 1s in front.

Third place was claimed by Force India's Perez after he chased and passed team-mate Nico Hulkenberg.

Daniel Ricciardo's strong form in the season's early rounds continued at Sakhir when he left team-mate Sebastian Vettel in the shade again. Not only did the Australian outqualify his more illustrious team-mate, third versus 11th, but he overtook him late in the race as he headed to fourth place.

Hulkenberg finished fifth, just ahead of Vettel, but that position had looked set to be claimed by Jenson Button until his McLaren was struck by clutch problems.

Ferrari's troubled start grew worse in Bahrain as they struggled for straightline speed and Fernando Alonso and Kimi Raikkonen could finish only ninth and 10th.

The race's most spectacular collision was the one between Pastor Maldonado and Esteban Gutierrez. The Venezuelan rejoined the circuit after a pitstop and tried to take the inside line into Turn 1 just as the Mexican turned in, which pitched Gutierrez's Sauber into a barrel roll. Maldonado was then given a stop/go penalty, three points on his competition licence and a five-place grid penalty for the next race.

Lewis Hamilton shone in the dark as he won what he described as "a real racers' race".

SAKHIR ROUND 3

DATE: **6 APRIL 2014**

Laps: **57** • Distance: **191.539 miles/308.253km** • Weather: **Dark and dry**

Pos	Driver	Team	Result	Stops	Qualifying Time	Grid
1	**Lewis Hamilton**	Mercedes	1h39m42.743s	2	1m33.464s	2
2	**Nico Rosberg**	Mercedes	1h39m43.828s	2	1m33.815s	1
3	**Sergio Perez**	Force India	1h40m06.810s	2	1m34.346s	4
4	**Daniel Ricciardo**	Red Bull	1h40m07.232s	2	1m34.051s	13*
5	**Nico Hulkenberg**	Force India	1h40m11.397s	2	1m35.116s	11
6	**Sebastian Vettel**	Red Bull	1h40m12.622s	2	1m34.985s	10
7	**Felipe Massa**	Williams	1h40m14.008s	3	1m34.511s	7
8	**Valtteri Bottas**	Williams	1h40m14.619s	3	1m34.247s	3
9	**Fernando Alonso**	Ferrari	1h40m15.338s	3	1m34.992s	9
10	**Kimi Raikkonen**	Ferrari	1h40m16.205s	3	1m34.368s	5
11	**Daniil Kyvat**	Toro Rosso	1h40m24.085s	3	1m35.145s	12
12	**Romain Grosjean**	Lotus	1h40m25.886s	3	1m35.908s	16
13	**Max Chilton**	Marussia	1h40m42.652s	3	1m37.913s	21
14	**Pastor Maldonado**	Lotus	1h40m45.546s	4	1m36.663s	17
15	**Kamui Kobayashi**	Caterham	1h41m10.643s	2	1m37.085s	18
16	**Jules Bianchi**	Marussia	56 laps	5	1m37.310s	19
17	**Jenson Button**	McLaren	55 laps	2	1m34.387s	6
R	**Kevin Magnussen**	McLaren	40 laps/clutch	3	1m34.712s	8
R	**Esteban Gutierrez**	Sauber	39 laps/accident	2	1m35.891s	15
R	**Marcus Ericsson**	Caterham	33 laps/oil leak	2	1m37.875s	20
R	**Jean-Eric Vergne**	Toro Rosso	18 laps/crash damage	2	1m35.286s	14
R	**Adrian Sutil**	Sauber	17 laps/accident	2	1m36.840s	22**

FASTEST LAP: ROSBERG, 1M37.020S, 124.787MPH/200.826KPH ON LAP 49 • RACE LEADERS: HAMILTON 1-18, 22-57; ROSBERG 19-21
* 10-PLACE GRID PENALTY FOR UNSAFE RELEASE,
** 5-PLACE GRID PENALTY FOR FORCING GROSJEAN OFF TRACK

CHINESE GP

Lewis Hamilton made it three wins in a row to take the championship lead from Mercedes GP team-mate Nico Rosberg, who finished a distant second. To many, though, the star of the race was Fernando Alonso who wrestled his Ferrari to third.

By making his opening stint of the race longer than those of his rivals, Lewis Hamilton opened out an advantage that he was never to lose. Indeed, the biggest surprise of the grand prix was when the chequered flag was shown a lap early, after 55 laps. As a result of this, the results were declared a lap earlier, after 54 laps.

What remained to be played out in Hamilton's wake was whether Mercedes would claim its third successive one-two finish. What stood between the team and this great achievement was Fernando Alonso and his Ferrari. The matter was sorted in Nico Rosberg's favour on lap 42, when he made good his ascent from a poor start caused by car telemetry failure, and passed the Spaniard three laps after his final pitstop.

Daniel Ricciardo was the highest finisher of the Red Bull Racing duo, coming home fourth to Sebastian Vettel's fifth. Had he not made a poor getaway, falling from second to fourth and thus losing out to Vettel and Alonso, the Australian might have even finished higher.

Then there was Felipe Massa. Starting sixth, he should have been in contention for a useful haul of points, but his FW36 was lightly damaged when hit on the opening lap by Alonso. Worse was to follow when his first pitstop was made far longer than planned as the pitcrew lost time by attempting to fit the rear tyres to the wrong corners of the car. He finished a disgruntled 15th.

Helped by this and a few other glitches, Nico Hulkenberg continued his scoring run by racing to sixth for Force India after managing to keep Valtteri Bottas's Williams at bay and thus re-establish himself ahead of Sergio Perez in the team pecking order.

Remarkably, Lotus - fourth overall in 2013 - left China still without scoring, Romain Grosjean being denied a probable 10th place by gearbox failure. Also out of the points, and suffering poor form, was McLaren, with Jenson Button finishing a lapped 11th.

SHANGHAI ROUND 4

Laps: 54 • Distance: 189.568 miles/305.081km • Weather: Dry and cloudy

DATE: 20 APRIL 2014

Pos	Driver	Team	Result	Stops	Qualifying Time	Grid
1	Lewis Hamilton	Mercedes	1h33m28.338s	2	1m53.860s	1
2	Nico Rosberg	Mercedes	1h33m46.400s	2	1m55.143s	4
3	Fernando Alonso	Ferrari	1h33m51.942s	2	1m55.637s	5
4	Daniel Ricciardo	Red Bull	1h33m55.474s	2	1m54.455s	2
5	Sebastian Vettel	Red Bull	1h34m16.116s	2	1m54.960s	3
6	Nico Hulkenberg	Force India	1h34m22.633s	2	1m56.366s	8
7	Valtteri Bottas	Williams	1h34m24.035s	2	1m56.282s	7
8	Kimi Raikkonen	Ferrari	1h34m44.673s	2	1m56.860s	11
9	Sergio Perez	Force India	1h34m50.985s	2	1m58.264s	16
10	Daniil Kvyat	Toro Rosso	53 laps	2	1m57.289s	13
11	Jenson Button	McLaren	53 laps	2	1m56.963s	12
12	Jean-Eric Vergne	Toro Rosso	53 laps	2	1m56.773s	9
13	Kevin Magnussen	McLaren	53 laps	2	1m57.675s	15
14	Pastor Maldonado	Lotus	53 laps	2	No time	22
15	Felipe Massa	Williams	53 laps	2	1m56.147s	6
16	Esteban Gutierrez	Sauber	53 laps	3	1m58.988s	17
17	Jules Bianchi	Marussia	53 laps	2	1m59.326s	19
18	Kamui Kobayashi	Caterham	53 laps	3	1m59.260s	18
19	Max Chilton	Marussia	52 laps	3	2m00.865s	21
20	Marcus Ericsson	Caterham	52 laps	3	2m00.646s	20
R	Romain Grosjean	Lotus	28 laps/gearbox	1	1m57.079s	10
R	Adrian Sutil	Sauber	5 laps/engine	0	1m57.397s	14

FASTEST LAP: **ROSBERG, 1M40.402S, 121.453MPH/195.460KPH ON LAP 39** • RACE LEADERS: **HAMILTON 1-54**

After third place in Bahrain, Sergio Perez had to make do with taking his Force India to ninth.

SPANISH GP

Lewis Hamilton and Mercedes GP team-mate Nico Rosberg ran different race strategies, but it all came together in the final two laps as Rosberg attacked Hamilton's lead. The British driver hung on to make it four wins on the trot, with Ricciardo the best of the rest.

Following frustration in Melbourne, Lewis Hamilton was the one to beat and success in Spain moved him three points ahead of Rosberg in the points table. However, the outcome was secured only by a dash to the finish line where Rosberg finished just 0.636s behind Hamilton.

Mercedes had filled the front row, Hamilton ahead of Rosberg, and this was still their track position as they exited the first corner – a poor getaway meant that the German wasn't able to make the most of the long run to Elf to line up for a passing move. So he tucked in behind and waited. Both had started on Pirelli's medium compound tyre and Rosberg appeared to treat his more kindly because he didn't pit until three laps after Hamilton. Then, in a roll of the dice, his pitcrew sent him out again on hard tyres, while Hamilton had opted for a second set of mediums. When they had made their final stops, Hamilton was ahead by 4.8s and Rosberg duly used his second set of mediums to close in as Hamilton lapped more slowly on his hard tyres. With four laps to go, Rosberg was within 1s and applying the pressure, but Hamilton did just enough to stay in front.

With no rival able to challenge Mercedes, Ricciardo finished 49s down in third, usurping Valtteri Bottas by making his first stop six laps earlier than the Finn and staying ahead when the Williams driver rejoined.

Although he finished one place adrift of his junior team-mate again, Sebastian Vettel can't have felt too disappointed with the speed he showed as he fought back from 15th, from where he had to start after a gearbox problem in Q3, and the way he passed Kimi Raikkonen and Bottas.

Even after scoring his first points of 2014, Romain Grosjean had reason for complaint: his eighth place was a couple of positions down on what It could have been because his Lotus was slowed by a problematic engine sensor.

Hamilton leads Rosberg and Bottas down the descent to the first corner on lap 1.

BARCELONA ROUND 5

DATE: **11 MAY 2014**

Laps: 66 • Distance: **190.904 miles/307.231km** • Weather: **Sunny & warm**

Pos	Driver	Team	Result	Stops	Qualifying Time	Grid
1	**Lewis Hamilton**	Mercedes	1h41m05.155s	2	1m25.232s	1
2	**Nico Rosberg**	Mercedes	1h41m05.791s	2	1m25.400s	2
3	**Daniel Ricciardo**	Red Bull	1h41m54.169s	2	1m26.285s	3
4	**Sebastian Vettel**	Red Bull	1h42m21.857s	3	No time	15*
5	**Valtteri Bottas**	Williams	1h42m24.448s	2	1m26.632s	4
6	**Fernando Alonso**	Ferrari	1h42m32.898s	3	1m27.140s	7
7	**Kimi Raikkonen**	Ferrari	65 laps	2	1m27.104s	6
8	**Romain Grosjean**	Lotus	65 laps	2	1m26.960s	5
9	**Sergio Perez**	Force India	65 laps	2	1m28.002s	11
10	**Nico Hulkenberg**	Force India	65 laps	2	1m27.685s	10
11	**Jenson Button**	McLaren	65 laps	2	1m27.335s	8
12	**Kevin Magnussen**	McLaren	65 laps	2	No time	14
13	**Felipe Massa**	Williams	65 laps	3	1m27.402s	9
14	**Daniil Kyvat**	Toro Rosso	65 laps	3	1m28.039s	12
15	**Pastor Maldonado**	Lotus	65 laps	2	No time	22
16	**Esteban Gutierrez**	Sauber	65 laps	3	1m28.280s	13
17	**Adrian Sutil**	Sauber	65 laps	2	1m28.563s	16
18	**Jules Bianchi**	Marussia	64 laps	2	1m30.177s	18
19	**Max Chilton**	Marussia	64 laps	3	1m29.586s	17
20	**Marcus Ericsson**	Caterham	64 laps	2	1m30.312s	19
R	**Kamui Kobayashi**	Caterham	34 laps/brakes	1	1m30.375s	20
R	**Jean-Eric Vergne**	Toro Rosso	24 laps/exhaust	1	No time	21**

FASTEST LAP: VETTEL, 1M28.918S, 117.112MPH/188.474KPH ON LAP 55 • RACE LEADERS: HAMILTON 1-17, 22-43, 46-66; ROSBERG 18-21, 44-45
* 5-PLACE GRID PENALTY FOR GEARBOX CHANGE,
** 10-PLACE GRID PENALTY

MONACO GP

When a championship battle is a two-horse race, the going can get rough and underlying tensions between the Mercedes GP drivers came to the surface in qualifying. Then Rosberg upset Hamilton further by leading him home in the race by 9s.

The initial upset came in final qualifying when Nico Rosberg had been a fraction faster than Lewis Hamilton on their first Q3 flying lap. Then, in the closing moments of his second flier, Rosberg was offline through Casino and shot up the escape road at Mirabeau. Out came the yellow flags and so Hamilton, behind him on the track, had to back off. He was livid, and let everyone know it, convinced not only that his final lap would have been good enough for his first Monaco pole, but that his team-mate had brought out the yellow flags on purpose.

At Monaco, of course, pole offers an excellent opportunity to be ahead out of the opening corner, Ste Devote, and thereafter it is notoriously hard for anyone to pass. So, once Rosberg had taken pole, Hamilton must have realized that his best chance had gone. It turned out to be his only chance, too, as the team elected not to change their tactics.

To add insult to injury, Hamilton then got dirt in one of his eyes and had to back off, allowing Daniel Ricciardo to close in for his second consecutive third-place finish.

Fourth place went to Fernando Alonso, despite his Ferrari's ERS playing up, and he still finished well clear of Nico Hulkenberg, who gained a place on the opening lap when team-mate Sergio Perez collided with Jenson Button's McLaren. Hulkenberg's best move of the race came when he passed the other McLaren, belonging to Kevin Magnussen, at Portier.

Perhaps the happiest driver of all was Jules Bianchi, who finished ninth to give Marussia its first score, with the two invaluable points propelling the team to ninth in the constructors' table.

Bianchi's team-mate Max Chilton found himself in the wars, clipping Kimi Raikkonen's third-placed Ferrari as he followed safety car procedure to unlap himself. This sent the Finn to the pits to have a flat right rear replaced, but he failed to make it back to the top 10.

MONACO ROUND 6

DATE: **25 MAY 2014**

Laps: **78** • Distance: **161.887 miles/260.532km** • Weather: **Warm & sunny**

Pos	Driver	Team	Result	Stops	Qualifying Time	Grid
1	**Nico Rosberg**	Mercedes	1h49m27.661s	1	1m15.989s	1
2	**Lewis Hamilton**	Mercedes	1h49m36.871s	1	1m16.048s	2
3	**Daniel Ricciardo**	Red Bull	1h49m37.275s	1	1m16.384s	3
4	**Fernando Alonso**	Ferrari	1h50m00.113s	1	1m16.686s	5
5	**Nico Hulkenberg**	Force India	77 laps	1	1m17.846s	11
6	**Jenson Button**	McLaren	77 laps	1	1m17.988s	12
7	**Felipe Massa**	Williams	77 laps	1	No time	16
8	**Romain Grosjean**	Lotus	77 laps	2	1m18.196s	14
9	**Jules Bianchi**	Marussia	77 laps	1	1m19.332s	21*
10	**Kevin Magnussen**	McLaren	77 laps	1	1m17.555s	8
11	**Marcus Ericsson**	Caterham	77 laps	2	1m21.732s	22**
12	**Kimi Raikkonen**	Ferrari	77 laps	3	1m17.389s	6
13	**Kamui Kobayashi**	Caterham	75 laps	2	1m20.133s	20
14	**Max Chilton**	Marussia	75 laps	3	1m19.928s	19
R	**Esteban Gutierrez**	Sauber	59 laps/spun off	1	1m18.741s	17
R	**Valtteri Bottas**	Williams	55 laps/engine	1	1m18.082s	13
R	**Jean-Eric Vergne**	Toro Rosso	50 laps/exhaust	2	1m17.540s	7
R	**Adrian Sutil**	Sauber	23 laps/spun off	1	1m18.745s	18
R	**Daniil Kyvat**	Toro Rosso	10 laps/exhaust	0	1m18.090s	9
R	**Sebastian Vettel**	Red Bull	5 laps/turbocharger	1	1m16.547s	4
R	**Sergio Perez**	Force India	0 laps/collision	0	1m18.327s	10
NS	**Pastor Maldonado**	Lotus	0 laps/fuel pump	0	1m18.356s	15

FASTEST LAP: RAIKKONEN, 1M18.479S, 95.206MPH/153.219KPH ON LAP 75 • RACE LEADERS: ROSBERG 1-78
* 5-PLACE GRID PENALTY FOR GEARBOX CHANGE
** MADE TO START FROM REAR OF GRID FOR CAUSING A COLLISION

Nico Rosberg leads into Ste Devote and, as is the way in Monaco, was never headed again.

A smile is seldom far from Daniel Ricciardo's face, but his beam went on forever on this June night in Montreal as his late charge took him past Nico Rosberg's power-sapped Mercedes for his first grand prix win.

This was a race that wasn't so much a case of Red Bull Racing rediscovering its winning touch, but one in which Mercedes had a technical nightmare after early domination.

Nico Rosberg led away from pole and Lewis Hamilton was jumped by Sebastian Vettel as he looked to find a way past Rosberg into the first corner. However, Hamilton was soon back into second and closed in on his team-mate.

Mid-race, after trying for laps to unsettle Rosberg, Hamilton lost pace, his Mercedes' MGU-K having failed. Amazingly, at the start of the very next lap, Rosberg's car was affected by a similar problem. They both continued, but at an abated pace and Hamilton was able to emerge from their second pitstops ahead, only for his rear brakes to fail on his out lap.

Rosberg was thus left with a clear lead but Sergio Perez was catching the Mercedes' driver in his Force India after running a one-stop strategy. Although the Mexican closed in, he never got to within 1s and so wasn't able to activate his DRS to help him line up a passing manoeuvre. Then, with his brakes past their best, Perez was unable to keep Ricciardo behind him, the Australian moving past him around the outside at Turn 1 on lap 66. Two laps later, Vettel went past him too.

By this point, Ricciardo had hit the front, with Rosberg unable to offer any resistance to the DRS-assisted move. He at least had enough in hand to hold onto second place, from Vettel.

However, there was still drama to come: going into the final lap, Massa lined up a move on Perez into Turn 1 and their cars touched, spitting both into the barriers. Massa was furious, convinced that Perez had driven across him as he tried to go past.

As a result of this, Jenson Button's run to fourth place was hardly noticed, but he had climbed from eight to sixth by using his McLaren's DRS and then gained two more places when Massa and Perez clashed.

98

Daniel Ricciardo had every reason to smile on the podium after securing his first F1 victory.

MONTREAL ROUND 7
DATE: **8 JUNE 2014**

Laps: **70** • Distance: **189.686 miles/305.271km** • Weather: **Hot & sunny**

Pos	Driver	Team	Result	Stops	Qualifying Time	Grid
1	**Daniel Ricciardo**	Red Bull	1h39m12.830s	2	1m15.589s	6
2	**Nico Rosberg**	Mercedes	1h39m17.066s	2	1m14.874s	1
3	**Sebastian Vettel**	Red Bull	1h39m18.077s	2	1m15.548s	3
4	**Jenson Button**	McLaren	1h39m24.585s	2	1m16.182s	9
5	**Nico Hulkenberg**	Force India	1h39m25.673s	1	1m16.300s	11
6	**Fernando Alonso**	Ferrari	1h39m27.699s	2	1m15.814s	7
7	**Valtteri Bottas**	Williams	1h39m36.408s	2	1m15.550s	4
8	**Jean-Eric Vergne**	Toro Rosso	1h39m40.856s	2	1m16.162s	8
9	**Kevin Magnussen**	McLaren	1h39m42.084s	2	1m16.310s	12
10	**Kimi Raikkonen**	Ferrari	1h40m06.508s	2	1m16.214s	10
11	**Sergio Perez**	Force India	69 laps/collision	1	1m16.472s	13
12	**Felipe Massa**	Williams	69 laps/collision	2	1m15.578s	5
13	**Adrian Sutil**	Sauber	69 laps	2	1m117.314s	16
14	**Esteban Gutierrez**	Sauber	64 laps/power unit	3	No time	22
R	**Romain Grosjean**	Lotus	59 laps/rear wing	2	1m16.687s	14
R	**Daniil Kvyat**	Toro Rosso	47 laps/transmission	2	1m16.713s	15
R	**Lewis Hamilton**	Mercedes	46 laps/brakes	2	1m14.953s	2
R	**Kamui Kobayashi**	Caterham	23 laps/suspension	0	1m19.278s	21*
R	**Pastor Maldonado**	Lotus	21 laps/power unit	0	1m18.328s	17
R	**Marcus Ericsson**	Caterham	7 laps/power unit	0	1m19.820s	20
R	**Max Chilton**	Marussia	0 laps/collision	0	1m18.348s	18
R	**Jules Bianchi**	Marussia	0 laps/collision	0	1m18.359s	19

FASTEST LAP: MASSA, 1M18.504S, 124.270MPH/199.994KPH ON LAP 58 • RACE LEADERS: ROSBERG 1-17, 19-43, 48-67; HAMILTON 18, 44-45; MASSA 46-47; RICCIARDO 68-70
* 5-PLACE GRID PENALTY FOR GEARBOX CHANGE

AUSTRIAN GP

Formula One's return to what had been the A1-Ring was a successful one and Nico Rosberg had reason to smile as he raced to his third win of 2014, with Lewis Hamilton making it to second from ninth.

Now known as the Red Bull Ring, the track had not changed since F1 last visited in 2003, although the injection of cash from the energy drink giant had upgraded the facilities. It was great to be back at this scenic circuit, and the team that set the pace in qualifying was not Mercedes GP but Williams, with Felipe Massa and Valtteri Bottas locking out the front row.

Rosberg qualified just behind them, but team-mate Hamilton spun, leaving him ninth.

The big question was whether Williams could maintain this form in the race – and the answer was that they could. However, it wasn't to be their day: a perhaps too-cautious approach left their drivers just short of their target.

Although Massa led away and Bottas ran behind him for the first 14 laps until they pitted, Rosberg had come in earlier, on lap 11, and was in front once Force India's Sergio Perez finally came in for his first stop to change from the harder compound tyre. From there, Rosberg was in control: the Williams duo was unable to respond as Hamilton came past them, with Bottas clinching his first podium result by finishing third and Massa another 9s back in fourth. Afterwards, Williams' head of vehicle performance, Rob Smedley, suggested that the Mercedes had had superior pace all along but simply not shown it in Q3 and added that he was pleased with the third and fourth place points haul.

Fifth went to Fernando Alonso, giving his all as usual for Ferrari to finish 10s up on Perez, who had every reason to rue starting the race back in 15th, due to a five-place grid penalty imposed for his last-lap clash with Massa in Montreal.

Red Bull's hopes of a good result on home ground were denied as Daniel Ricciardo's eighth-place finish was the best it could manage, after Sebastian Vettel pulled out with an electronic problem that had dropped him to the tail of the field. By stopping, he at least saved engine life.

RED BULL RING ROUND 8

DATE: 22 JUNE 2014

Laps: **71** • Distance: **190.851 miles/307.145km** • Weather: **Warm and bright**

Pos	Driver	Team	Result	Stops	Qualifying Time	Grid
1	Nico Rosberg	Mercedes	1h27m54.976s	2	1m08.944s	3
2	Lewis Hamilton	Mercedes	1h27m56.908s	2	No time	9
3	Valtteri Bottas	Williams	1h28m03.148s	2	1m08.846s	2
4	Felipe Massa	Williams	1h28m12.334s	2	1m08.769s	1
5	Fernando Alonso	Ferrari	1h28m13.529s	2	1m09.285s	4
6	Sergio Perez	Force India	1h28m23.522s	2	1m09.754s	15*
7	Kevin Magnussen	McLaren	1h28m27.007s	2	1m09.515s	6
8	Daniel Ricciardo	Red Bull	1h28m38.498s	2	1m09.466s	5
9	Nico Hulkenberg	Force India	1h28m39.113s	2	No time	10
10	Kimi Raikkonen	Ferrari	1h28m42.753s	2	1m10.795s	8
11	Jenson Button	McLaren	1h28m45.942s	2	1m09.780s	11
12	Pastor Maldonado	Lotus	70 laps	2	1m09.939s	13
13	Adrian Sutil	Sauber	70 laps	2	1m10.825s	16
14	Romain Grosjean	Lotus	70 laps	2	1m10.642s	PL
15	Jules Bianchi	Marussia	69 laps	1	1m11.412s	18
16	Kamui Kobayashi	Caterham	69 laps	1	1m11.673s	19
17	Max Chilton	Marussia	69 laps	1	1m11.775s	21**
18	Marcus Ericsson	Caterham	69 laps	2	1m12.673s	20
19	Esteban Gutierrez	Sauber	69 laps	3	1m11.349s	17
R	Jean-Eric Vergne	Toro Rosso	59 laps/brakes	2	1m10.073s	14
R	Sebastian Vettel	Red Bull	34 laps/pulled out	2	1m09.801s	12
R	Daniil Kvyat	Toro Rosso	24 laps/suspension	1	1m09.619s	7

FASTEST LAP: PEREZ, 1M12.142S, 134.138MPH/215.874KPH ON LAP 59 • RACE LEADERS: MASSA 1-13, 42; BOTTAS 14-15, 41; PEREZ 16-26; ROSBERG 27-40, 48-71; ALONSO 43-47
* 5-PLACE GRID PENALTY FOR CANADIAN GP COLLISION
** 3-PLACE GRID PENALTY FOR CANADIAN GP COLLISION, PL STARTED F4ROM PITLANE AFTER GEARBOX CHANGE

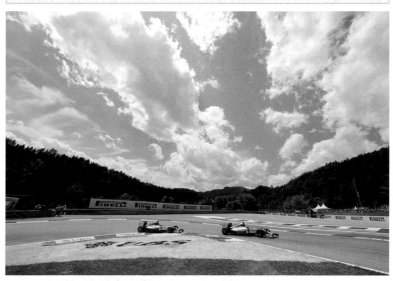

Lewis Hamilton harried Nico Rosberg in the closing laps but just couldn't find a way past.

This was a victory that meant a huge amount to Lewis Hamilton. Not just because it was only his second British GP win but because he'd had to advance from sixth on the grid. Whether he'd have got past Nico Rosberg, whose gearbox broke, became academic.

Lewis Hamilton was almost speechless after qualifying as he staggered, looking stunned, to face the TV interviewers. He had dropped the ball in a big way by electing not to stay out for the final lap as the track dried. Few had thought that it would dry enough for their times to improve, but Hamilton didn't even try and was caught out when conditions improved markedly. So, instead of starting his home race from pole position, he would have Rosberg, Sebastian Vettel, Jenson Button, Nico Hulkenberg and Kevin Magnussen all ahead of him.

With the Mercedes F1 W05 still very much the pick of the bunch, Hamilton was always likely to work his way up the order, but the question was how big Rosberg's lead would be while he did it.

Hamilton received no help from Vettel, who failed to get pass Rosberg at the start. Indeed, the German went backwards rather than forwards, being demoted by Button and Magnussen as well as Hamilton, who jumped Hulkenberg and then passed Vettel.

Moments later though, the safety car was required because Kimi Raikkonen had run wide out of Aintree, then lost control of his Ferrari as he attempted to rejoin the circuit, slamming into the barriers and bouncing back into the path of Felipe Massa's Williams.

Once released to race again, Hamilton wasted no time in passing the McLarens, and chased after Rosberg. Running different strategies, with Rosberg pitting much earlier, Hamilton closed in. Then Rosberg's gearbox, which had been being playing up since lap 20, cried enough and he was out.

With no challengers, Hamilton raced to his second British GP win. Valtteri Bottas landed what was a great second place, particularly as he had had to start 14th after being caught out by the rain in qualifying. Daniel Ricciardo finished third, but Button was closing in so quickly that he would have needed only one more lap to have made it to third and his first British GP podium.

Lewis Hamilton was in a class of his own, winning his home grand prix by half a minute.

SILVERSTONE ROUND 9

DATE: **6 JULY 2014**

Laps: **52** • Distance: **190.271 miles/306.212km** • Weather: **Warm & sunny**

Pos	Driver	Team	Result	Stops	Qualifying Time	Grid
1	**Lewis Hamilton**	Mercedes	2h26m52.094s	2	1m38.232s	6
2	Valtteri Bottas	Williams	2h27m22.229s	1	1m45.318s	14
3	Daniel Ricciardo	Red Bull	2h27m38.959s	1	1m40.606s	8
4	Jenson Button	McLaren	2h27m39.484s	1	1m38.200s	3
5	Sebastian Vettel	Red Bull	2h27m45.958s	2	1m37.386s	2
6	Fernando Alonso	Ferrari	2h27m52.040s	1	1m45.935s	16
7	Kevin Magnussen	McLaren	2h27m54.657s	1	1m38.417s	5
8	Nico Hulkenberg	Force India	2h28m20.786s	1	1m38.329s	4
9	Daniil Kvyat	Toro Rosso	2h28m21.434s	2	1m40.707s	9
10	Jean-Eric Vergne	Toro Rosso	51 laps	1	1m40.855s	10
11	Sergio Perez	Force India	51 laps	1	1m40.457s	7
12	Romain Grosjean	Lotus	51 laps	1	1m38.496s	11
13	Adrian Sutil	Sauber	51 laps	1	No time	13
14	Jules Bianchi	Marussia	51 laps	1	1m38.709s	12
15	Kamui Kobayashi	Caterham	50 laps	2	1m49.625s	22
16	Max Chilton	Marussia	50 laps	3	1m39.800s	17*
17	Pastor Maldonado	Lotus	49 laps	1	1m44.018s*	20**
R	Nico Rosberg	Mercedes	28 laps/gearbox	1	1m35.766s	1
R	Marcus Ericsson	Caterham	11 laps/suspension	0	1m49.321s	21
R	Esteban Gutierrez	Sauber	9 laps/accident	0	1m40.912s	19!
R	Felipe Massa	Williams	1 lap/accident	0	1m45.695s	15
R	Kimi Raikkonen	Ferrari	0 laps/accident	0	1m46.684s	18

FASTEST LAP: HAMILTON, 1M37.176S, 135.614MPH/218.250KPH ON LAP 26 • RACE LEADERS: ROSBERG 1-18, 25-28; HAMILTON 19-24, 29-52
* 5-PLACE GRID PENALTY FOR GEARBOX CHANGE,
** TIME DISALLOWED FOR FUEL INFRINGEMENT • ! 15-PLACE GRID PENALTY FOR GEARBOX CHANGE & UNSAFE RELEASE IN CANADIAN GP

GERMAN GP

Nico Rosberg matched Lewis Hamilton's home win at Silverstone by triumphing at Hockenheim, helped by his team-mate suffering brake failure and crashing out of qualifying, before charging from 20th to third in the race.

Hockenheim's grandstands were unusually empty for qualifying, but the cheer was still loud when a car speared into the barriers. The cheer wasn't very sporting, but it was partially understandable because the driver who had gone off was Hamilton. This meant that the British driver wouldn't escape Q2, which would give home driver Rosberg a clear shot at pole. He duly took top spot by 0.219s from Valtteri Bottas's Williams and, with Hamilton set to line up 19 places back on the grid, having been demoted an extra five places because of a gearbox change, Rosberg's hopes of extending his points lead from four were hugely enhanced.

Felipe Massa clashed with Kevin Magnussen's McLaren at the first corner and rolled in an incident that brought out the safety car.

Then the race settled down and Rosberg pulled away. However, with Mercedes's performance advantage, Hamilton was up to second by lap 16 and then stayed out as others pitted. Hamilton didn't call at the pits until lap 26, by which time Bottas's Williams, on fresher tyres, had pushed him back to third.

On rejoining, he was eighth, but Hamilton then overtook Ricciardo – and Button, diving up the inside into the hairpin, only to discover that Button hadn't taken the wider entry line to let him through. The two clashed and the Mercedes' front wing was bent. Hamilton then passed Hulkenberg and gained three more places when Alonso, Vettel and Bottas pitted, but was immediately back behind the trio when he came in a lap after the Finn. And since Bottas had now completed all his pitstops, he stayed ahead of Hamilton, whose damaged front wing forced him into a three-stop strategy. Hamilton ended up third after Adrian Sutil abandoned his Sauber in the middle of the final corner. Despite the clear danger, no safety car appeared and since the field did not bunch up, Hamilton's chance to challenge Bottas and Rosberg was gone.

HOCKENHEIM ROUND 10

DATE: **20 JULY 2014**

Laps: **67** • Distance: **190.424 miles/306.458km** • Weather: **Warm and overcast**

Pos	Driver	Team	Result	Stops	Qualifying Time	Grid
1	Nico Rosberg	Mercedes	1h33m42.914s	2	1m16.540s	1
2	Valtteri Bottas	Williams	1h34m03.703s	2	1m16.759s	2
3	Lewis Hamilton	Mercedes	1h34m05.444s	3	No time	20*
4	Sebastian Vettel	Red Bull	1h34m26.928s	3	1m17.577s	6
5	Fernando Alonso	Ferrari	1h34m35.381s	3	1m17.649s	7
6	Daniel Ricciardo	Red Bull	1h34m35.463s	3	1m17.273s	5
7	Nico Hulkenberg	Force India	1h34m47.092s	2	1m18.014s	9
8	Jenson Button	McLaren	1h35m07.625s	3	1m18.193s	11
9	Kevin Magnussen	McLaren	66 laps	3	1m17.214s	4
10	Sergio Perez	Force India	66 laps	3	1m18.035s	10
11	Kimi Raikkonen	Ferrari	66 laps	3	1m18.273s	12
12	Pastor Maldonado	Lotus	66 laps	2	1m20.195s	18
13	Jean-Eric Vergne	Toro Rosso	66 laps	3	1m18.285s	13
14	Esteban Gutierrez	Sauber	66 laps	3	1m18.787s	16**
15	Jules Bianchi	Marussia	66 laps	3	1m19.676s	17
16	Kamui Kobayashi	Caterham	65 laps	3	1m20.408s	19
17	Max Chilton	Marussia	65 laps	3	1m20.489s	21
18	Marcus Ericsson	Caterham	65 laps	3	No time	22!
R	Adrian Sutil	Sauber	47 laps/spun off	3	1m19.142s	15
R	Daniil Kvyat	Toro Rosso	44 laps/ignition	2	1m17.965s	8
R	Romain Grosjean	Lotus	26 laps/overheating	1	1m18.983s	14
R	Felipe Massa	Williams	0 laps/collision	0	1m17.078s	3

FASTEST LAP: **HAMILTON, 1M19.908S, 128.043MPH/206.066KPH ON LAP 53** • RACE LEADERS: **ROSBERG 1-67**
* 5-PLACE GRID PENALTY FOR GEARBOX CHANGE,
** 3-PLACE GRID PENALTY FOR BRITISH GP COLLISION • ! HAD TO START FROM PITLANE AS CAR MODIFIED IN PARC FERME

Valtteri Bottas kept his Williams ahead of Lewis Hamilton to claim another second place.

HUNGARIAN GP

This was the outstanding race of the first half of the 2014 season. Winner Daniel Ricciardo hit the front with only two laps to go – up from the back of the grid – and Nico Rosberg was livid when Lewis Hamilton ignored team orders.

The pendulum of fortune swung in Rosberg's favour again when Hamilton had his car catch fire after a fuel line came loose before he had set a qualifying time. He would thus have to start from the rear of the grid (he eventually started from the pitlane, along with McLaren's Kevin Magnussen, as both had to have new cars built up for them). With overtaking a rarity at the Hungaroring, Mercedes was going to have to be very clever with its tactics, and Hamilton controlled in his attack, to claw back some points.

On a wet track, Rosberg eased clear of Valtteri Bottas, who had gone around the outside of Sebastian Vettel at Turn 1. Through the early laps, the only driver gaining places was Hamilton, who had spun at Turn 2 on lap 1, then got his head down and advanced to 13th when Marcus Ericsson crashed, which triggered a safety car period.

This hurt the first four runners, as they had passed the pit entrance. Jenson Button was the first in, followed by Daniel Ricciardo. They emerged in reverse order and were first and second when Rosberg, Bottas, Vettel and Alonso pitted a lap later. When the safety car withdrew, Button passed Ricciardo for the lead, but he had been sent out on another set of intermediates that were soon wrecked as the track dried, forcing him to pit for slicks and so elevating Felipe Massa to second.

Then came another safety car period after Sergio Perez crashed at the final corner. Ricciardo pitted and emerged sixth. This put Fernando Alonso into the lead, followed by Jean-Eric Vergne, but what shaped the race was the fact that Rosberg planned to pit twice more, Hamilton just once. Rosberg soon caught Hamilton and on lap 45 Hamilton was instructed to let him past, but refused.

Into the final few laps, Alonso led from Ricciardo and Hamilton, with Rosberg catching them fast. He got back onto Hamilton's tail but couldn't find a way past. Then, with three laps to go, Ricciardo passed Alonso into Turn 1 and the race was his.

Daniel Ricciardo overtakes Fernando Alonso to take the lead with just three laps to go.

HUNGARORING ROUND 11

DATE: **27 JULY 2014**

Laps: **70** • Distance: **190.531 miles/306.631km** • Weather: **Warm and wet but drying**

Pos	Driver	Team	Result	Stops	Qualifying Time	Grid
1	**Daniel Ricciardo**	Red Bull	1h53m05.058s	3	1m23.391s	4
2	**Fernando Alonso**	Ferrari	1h53m10.283s	2	1m23.909s	5
3	**Lewis Hamilton**	Mercedes	1h53m10.915s	2	No time	22*
4	**Nico Rosberg**	Mercedes	1h53m11.419s	3	1m22.715s	1
5	**Felipe Massa**	Williams	1h53m34.899s	3	1m24.223s	6
6	**Kimi Raikkonen**	Ferrari	1h53m36.549s	2	1m26.792s	16
7	**Sebastian Vettel**	Red Bull	1h53m46.022s	2	1m23.201s	2
8	**Valtteri Bottas**	Williams	1h53m46.402s	3	1m23.354s	3
9	**Jean-Eric Vergne**	Toro Rosso	1h54m03.585s	2	1m24.720s	8
10	**Jenson Button**	McLaren	1h54m12.338s	3	1m24.294s	7
11	**Adrian Sutil**	Sauber	1h54m13.227s	2	1m25.136s	11
12	**Kevin Magnussen**	McLaren	1h54m23.523s	2	No time	21*
13	**Pastor Maldonado**	Lotus	1h54m29.082s	3	No time	20**
14	**Daniil Kvyat**	Toro Rosso	69 laps	2	1m24.706s	10
15	**Jules Bianchi**	Marussia	69 laps	3	1m27.419s	15
16	**Max Chilton**	Marussia	69 laps	2	1m27.819s	18
R	**Esteban Gutierrez**	Sauber	32 laps/power unit	1	1m25.260s	13
R	**Kamui Kobayashi**	Caterham	24 laps/fuel system	1	1m27.139s	17
R	**Sergio Perez**	Force India	22 laps/accident	1	1m25.211s	12
R	**Nico Hulkenberg**	Force India	14 laps/collision	1	1m24.775s	9
R	**Romain Grosjean**	Lotus	10 laps/accident	1	1m25.337s	14
R	**Marcus Ericsson**	Caterham	7 laps/accident	0	1m28.643s	19

FASTEST LAP: ROSBERG, 1M25.724S, 114.320MPH/183.981KPH ON LAP 64 • RACE LEADERS: ROSBERG 1-9, RICCIARDO 10-13, 15-23, 39-54, 68-70, BUTTON 14, ALONSO 24-37, 55-67, HAMILTON 38
* MADE TO START FROM PITLANE FOR CHANGING GEARBOX UNDER PARC FERME CONDITIONS
** 5-PLACE GRID PENALTY FOR GEARBOX CHANGE

BELGIAN GP

The summer break might have refreshed the teams, but controversy reared its head when Nico Rosberg clashed with Leiws Hamilton on the second lap, taking him out, then declared that it had been intentional. As a result, Daniel Ricciardo won the day.

The fact that one Mercedes took the other out infuriated the Mercedes GP management. When a team is dominant, it ought to be a matter simply of which driver finishes first, and which second. Of course, no self-respecting driver ever wants to finish second to a team-mate, and after Rosberg attempted a passing move into Les Combes on lap 2 but failed, he decided to keep his nose in there anyway, to send a message to Hamilton.

The result was that the German's front right wing slashed the English racer's left rear tyre and dropped him down the order. Despite damage to his front wing, Rosberg took the lead, but his pace was compromised. This let Daniel Ricciardo take over on lap 8 when Rosberg pitted for a new nose, the Australian having passed both Fernando Alonso and his Red Bull team-mate Sebastian Vettel. Valtteri Bottas led for a lap after Ricciardo pitted before the Red Bull driver took over again.

Ricciardo then led for the rest of the race to record the third win of his campaign, while Rosberg was able to make it back to second place, making notable progress in his final stint on the soft tyres to ensure that he usurped Bottas and Kimi Raikkonen before closing in on Riciardo. This was by far Raikkonen's best drive to this point. Had he had better top speed, he'd probably have been able to resist Bottas's attack and hold on to third.

The best battle of the day was over fifth as the McLarens and Alonso attacked Vettel, with the German holding on.

After Rosberg's post-race admission that he had chosen not to avoid contact, many started reconsidering whether his slip-up in qualifying at Monaco, which scuppered Hamilton's final run, had been deliberate too. However, the outcome at Spa was that he stretched his championship lead, to 29. Toto Wolff later described Rosberg's behaviour as "unacceptable".

SPA-FRANCHORCHAMPS ROUND 12 DATE: 24 AUGUST 2014

Laps: **44** • Distance: **191.414 miles/308.052km** • Weather: **Hot & sunny**

Pos	Driver	Team	Result	Stops	Qualifying Time	Grid
1	Daniel Ricciardo	Red Bull	1h24m36.556s	2	2m07.911s.	5
2	Nico Rosberg	Mercedes	1h24m39.939s	3	2m05.591s	1
3	Valtteri Bottas	Williams	1h25m04.588s	2	2m08.049s	6
4	Kimi Raikkonen	Ferrari	1h25m13.371s	2	2m08.780s	8
5	Sebastian Vettel	Red Bull	1h25m28.752s	3	2m07.717s	3
6	Jenson Button	McLaren	1h25m31.136s	2	2m09.776s	10
7	Fernando Alonso	Ferrari	1h25m37.718s	2	2m07.786s	4
8	Sergio Perez	Force India	1h25m40.849s	2	2m10.084s	13
9	Daniil Kvyat	Toro Rosso	1h25m41.903s	2	2m09.377s	11
10	Nico Hulkenberg	Force India	1h25m42.253s	2	2m11.267s	18
11	Jean-Eric Vergne	Toro Rosso	1h25m48.476s	2	2m09.805s	12
12	Kevin Magnussen	McLaren	1h25m50.818s*	2	2m08.679s	7
13	Felipe Massa	Williams	1h25m52.531s	3	2m09.178s	9
14	Adrian Sutil	Sauber	1h25m59.003s	3	2m10.328s	14
15	Esteban Gutierrez	Sauber	1h26m07.381s	2	2m13.414s	20
16	Max Chilton	Marussia	43 laps	2	2m12.566s	19
17	Marcus Ericsson	Caterham	43 laps	2	2m14.438s	22
18	Jules Bianchi	Marussia	39 laps/Gearbox	2	2m12.470s	16
R	Lewis Hamilton	Mercedes	38 laps/Handling	3	2m05.819s	2
R	Romain Grosjean	Lotus	33 laps/Handling	3	2m11.087s	15
R	Pastor Maldonado	Lotus	1 lap/Exhaust	0	2m11.261s	17
R	Andre Lotterer	Caterham	1 lap/Power unit	0	2m13.469s	21

FASTEST LAP:W ROSBERG, 1M50.511S, 141.772MPH/228.161KPH ON LAP 36 • RACE LEADERS: HAMILTON 1; ROSBERG 2–7; BOTTAS 12; RICCIARDO 8–11, 13–44
* 20 SECOND PENALTY FOR FORCING ALONSO OFF THE TRACK

This is the moment on lap 2 when Rosberg left his car's nose where Hamilton would hit it.

This was Lewis Hamilton at his best. Seeking to put one over Nico Rosberg after their clash at Spa-Francorchamps, he recovered from a bad start, hunted the German down and pressured him into a mistake before motoring on for victory.

Qualifying on pole after suffering mechanical problems in practice lifted Lewis Hamilton's spirits. It seemed to rebalance his psyche after the spat with team-mate Nico Rosberg, who had deliberately clipped him in the Belgian GP. The two men had been forced to attend a team meeting, where Rosberg had the riot act read to him.

That just left the race, and it all appeared to go wrong for Hamilton when his car failed him and he was unable to engage the right engine mode for the start. Slow away, he fell to fourth as Rosberg moved into the lead, followed by a fast-starting Kevin Magnussen, up from fifth, and Felipe Massa.

Hamilton knew he had to get past them, or Rosberg would be able to escape to extend his points advantage. So he grabbed the opportunity to get ahead of Magnussen when the Dane had been pressured and passed by Massa's Williams, slipping by out of the second chicane on lap 5. Five laps later, Hamilton passed Massa for second.

Hamilton then had to close in on Rosberg, which he did, being 1.7s behind before they pitted on consecutive laps. As this was planned to be their only stop, Hamilton was going to have to make his move out on the circuit. Within two laps of their stops, Hamilton got within DRS range. He then applied the pressure and, on lap 29, Rosberg slipped up, going straight on at the first chicane. Hamilton was through and motored off to win. Some talked of it having been an intentional move by Rosberg to atone for his Spa manoeuvre, but the team gave short shrift to that suggestion.

Valtteri Bottas's start was even worse than Hamilton's, dropping him to 10th by the first chicane. He then worked his way back up the order on a track that suited Williams, but he had to settle for fourth Massa, followed in by the Red Bulls of Daniel Ricciardo and Sebastian Vettel. Magnussen fell back to seventh, only to be demoted to 10th by a 5s penalty for forcing Bottas off the track.

Hamilton was delighted to have taken victory after pressuring Rosberg into a mistake.

MONZA ROUND 13

DATE: **7 SEPTEMBER 2014**

Laps: **53** • Distance: **190.596 miles/306.735km** • Weather: **Hot & sunny**

Pos	Driver	Team	Result	Stops	Qualifying Time	Grid
1	**Lewis Hamilton**	Mercedes	1h19m10.236s	1	1m24.109s	1
2	**Nico Rosberg**	Mercedes	1h19m13.411s	1	1m24.383s	2
3	**Felipe Massa**	Williams	1h19m35.262s	1	1m24.865s	4
4	**Valtteri Bottas**	Williams	1h19m51.022s	1	1m24.697s	3
5	**Daniel Ricciardo**	Red Bull	1h20m00.545s	1	1m25.709s	9
6	**Sebastian Vettel**	Red Bull	1h20m10.201s	1	1m25.436s	8
7	**Sergio Perez**	Force India	1h20m12.754s	1	1m25.944s	10
8	**Jenson Button**	McLaren	1h20m13.299s	1	1m25.379s	6
9	**Kimi Raikkonen**	Ferrari	1h20m13.771s	1	1m26.110s	11
10	**Kevin Magnussen**	McLaren	1h20m16.407s***	1	1m25.314s	5
11	**Daniil Kvyat**	Toro Rosso	1h20m21.420s	1	1m26.070s	21*
12	**Nico Hulkenberg**	Force India	1h20m22.842s	1	1m26.279s	13
13	**Jean-Eric Vergne**	Toro Rosso	1h20m23.239s	1	1m26.157s	12
14	**Pastor Maldonado**	Lotus	52 laps	1	1m27.520s	16
15	**Adrian Sutil**	Sauber	52 laps	1	1m26.588s	14
16	**Romain Grosjean**	Lotus	52 laps	1	1m27.632s	17
17	**Kamui Kobayashi**	Caterham	52 laps	1	1m27.671s	18
18	**Jules Bianchi**	Marussia	52 laps	1	1m27.738s	19
19	**Marcus Ericsson**	Caterham	51 laps	1	1m28.562	22**
20	**Esteban Gutierrez**	Sauber	51 laps	3	1m26.692s	15
R	**Fernando Alonso**	Ferrari	28 laps/ERS	1	1m25.430s	7
R	**Max Chilton**	Marussia	5 laps/accident	0	1m28.247s	20

FASTEST LAP: HAMILTON, 1M28.004S, 147.256MPH/236.986KPH ON LAP 29 • RACE LEADERS: ROSBERG 1–23, 26–28; HAMILTON 24–25, 29–53
* 10-PLACE GRID PENALTY FOR ENGINE CHANGE • ** MADE TO START FROM PITLANE FOR IGNORING WAVED YELLOW FLAGS
*** 5 SECOND PENALTY FOR FORCING BOTTAS OFF THE TRACK

SINGAPORE GP

This was the grand prix in which the season turned around. Lewis Hamilton raced to victory, but Nico Rosberg was hit by electronic problems and had to retire, allowing Hamilton to gain 25 points and move into the championship lead.

Twenty-two points adrift heading to Singapore, Lewis Hamilton had to work for his win – and he came away no longer behind team-mate Nico Rosberg but three points ahead.

Hamilton had shaded Rosberg for pole, but the Red Bulls were close and so might be able to play a role, offering a hope that he would be able to take more than seven points off Rosberg if he could win. As it happens, he didn't have to rely on them: Rosberg's electronics on his steering wheel failed on the way to the grid, forcing him to start from the pitlane. Although the German's car did get to start, it was withdrawn after 13 laps when the Mercedes engineers couldn't fix it.

Hamilton's started well, but his three-stop plans were put into jeopardy when the safety car was called out on lap 31 after a collision between Sergio Perez and Adrian Sutil, and this meant that he had to sweat about his chances in the closing laps. While his rivals were able to change to just two stops, Hamilton had just changed to a second set of the supersoft tyres and thus would have to pit for a third time in order to run a stint on the harder tyre.

When Hamilton came back out after his final stop, he was just ahead of Ricciardo and Fernando Alonso but behind Sebastian Vettel. Of course, Hamilton was on fresh rubber while Vettel's was old, but he still had to choose his moment carefully. And he did, getting back at Turn 7 on the following lap. Once past, Hamilton stretched away to a clear win, while Vettel stretched the life of his ageing tyres enough to hold on to second ahead of his team-mate and Alonso, the trio finishing almost nose-to-tail.

Fifth place went to Felipe Massa, nursing his tyres from lap 22 to the finish. Jean-Eric Vergne was best of the rest, finishing sixth for Toro Rosso in a race that included great passes on Kimi Raikkonen and Valtteri Bottas, the latter losing sixth on the last lap when he locked up and flat-spotted his tyres, enabling five rivals to get past.

MARINA BAY ROUND 14

DATE: **21 SEPTEMBER 2014**

Laps: **60** • Distance: **188.749 miles/303.763km** • Weather: **Hot & humid**

Pos	Driver	Team	Result	Stops	Qualifying Time	Grid
1	**Lewis Hamilton**	Mercedes	2h00m04.795s	3	1m45.681s	1
2	**Sebastian Vettel**	Red Bull	2h00m18.329s	2	1m45.902s	4
3	**Daniel Ricciardo**	Red Bull	2h00m19.068s	2	1m45.854s	3
4	**Fernando Alonso**	Ferrari	2h00m20.184s	3	1m45.907s	5
5	**Felipe Massa**	Williams	2h00m46.956s	2	1m46.000s	6
6	**Jean-Eric Vergne**	Toro Rosso	2h01m01.596s**	3	1m46.989s	12
7	**Sergio Perez**	Force India	2h01m03.833s	4	1m47.575s	15
8	**Kimi Raikkonen**	Ferrari	2h01m05.436s	3	1m46.170s	7
9	**Nico Hulkenberg**	Force India	2h01m06.456s	3	1m47.308s	13
10	**Kevin Magnussen**	McLaren	2h01m07.025s	3	1m46.250s	9
11	**Valtteri Bottas**	Williams	2h01m09.860s	2	1m46.187s	8
12	**Pastor Maldonado**	Lotus	2h01m11.710s	4	1m49.063s	18
13	**Romain Grosjean**	Lotus	2h01m12.824s	3	1m47.812s	16
14	**Daniil Kvyat**	Toro Rosso	2h01m16.803s	3	1m47.362s	10
15	**Marcus Ericsson**	Caterham	2h01m38.983s	2	1m52.287s	22
16	**Jules Bianchi**	Marussia	2h01m39.338s	3	1m49.440s	19
17	**Max Chilton**	Marussia	59 laps	3	1m50.473s	21
R	**Jenson Button**	McLaren	52 laps/control unit	2	1m46.943s	11
R	**Adrian Stuil**	Sauber	40 laps/water leak	3	1m48.324s	17
R	**Esteban Gutierrez**	Sauber	17 laps/electrical	1	1m47.333s	14
R	**Nico Rosberg**	Williams	13 laps/electronics	0	1m45.688s	2*
R	**Kamui Kobayashi**	Caterham	0 laps/fire	0	1m50.405s	20

FASTEST LAP: **HAMILTON, 1M50.417S, 102.611MPH/165.137KPH ON LAP 39** • RACE LEADERS: **HAMILTON 1-26, 28-52, 54-60; RICCIARDO 27; VETTEL 53**
* STARTED FROM THE PITLANE
** 5S PENALTY FOR EXCEEDING TRACK LIMITS

Valtteri Bottas kept his Williams ahead of Lewis Hamilton to claim another second place.

JAPANESE GP

Victory helped Lewis Hamilton to stretch his championship advantage over his Mercedes team-mate Nico Rosberg to 10 points, but this rain-hit race will always be remembered as the one during which Marussia's Jules Bianchi suffered a dreadful head injury.

Wet weather has so often been a component of the Japanese GP, as the autumn can be capricious. In 2014, the weather declined on Saturday and it was wet on race day.

Nico Rosberg had qualified on pole, but he didn't have to face a challenge for the lead on the downhill rush to the first corner because the conditions were deemed too wet and the race started with the field following the safety car.

This stayed out for the first nine laps and, by the time it withdrew, Fernando Alonso had already parked up, retiring his Ferrari with an electrical problem. Rosberg then led from Hamilton and Valtteri Bottas. But the track was beginning to dry and Jenson Button brought his McLaren in straightaway from seventh to change to intermediate tyres, followed in two laps later by Bottas and Daniel Ricciardo.

The Mercedes drivers delayed their arrival at the pits, with Rosberg coming in on lap 13. Hamilton, due in the following lap, pressed on to see if he could steal the lead, but he ran wide at Spoon on his in-lap and blew the chance. After their pitstops, Hamilton cut Rosberg's advantage to nothing and was considering a move when he left his DRS open into Turn 1 on lap 27 and ran wide there. Yet, his pace was superior, so he was soon back up with Rosberg, who was suffering from oversteer. Then, on lap 29, Hamilton braved it around the outside of Turn 1 to take the lead. And that was that as he pulled away to what would become victory.

However, the race didn't run its full course and Hamilton was 15s clear on lap 42 in deteriorating conditions when Adrian Sutil spun off at Dunlop Curve. Double waved yellow flags were displayed there when, next time around, Jules Bianchi also hit a wet patch there and speared off at an angle to hit the tail of a recovery vehicle. It was immediately clear how serious his injuries were and the safety car deployed before the race was red-flagged a couple of laps later.

Heavy rain meant that the safety car had to be deployed to lead the cars around at the start.

SUZUKA ROUND 15

DATE: **5 OCTOBER 2014**

Laps: **44** • Distance: **158.752 miles/255.487km** • Weather: **Rain**

Pos	Driver	Team	Result	Stops	Qualifying Time	Grid
1	**Lewis Hamilton**	Mercedes	1h51m43.021s	3	1m32.703s	2
2	**Nico Rosberg**	Mercedes	1h51m52.201s	3	1m32.506s	1
3	**Sebastian Vettel**	Red Bull	1h52m12.143s	3	1m34.432s	9
4	**Daniel Ricciardo**	Red Bull	1h52m21.389s	3	1m34.075s	6
5	**Jenson Button**	McLaren	1h52m50.571s	4	1m34.317s	8
6	**Valtteri Bottas**	Williams	1h53m36.794s	3	1m33.128s	3
7	**Felipe Massa**	Williams	1h53m38.147s	3	1m33.527s	4
8	**Nico Hulkenberg**	Force India	1h53m38.969s	4	1m35.099s	13
9	**Jean-Eric Vergne**	Toro Rosso	1h53m50.659s	3	1m34.984s	20*
10	**Sergio Perez**	Force India	43 laps	4	1m35.089s	11
11	**Daniil Kvyat**	Toro Rosso	43 laps	4	1m35.092s	12
12	**Kimi Raikkonen**	Ferrari	43 laps	5	1m34.542s	10
13	**Esteban Gutierrez**	Sauber	43 laps	3	1m35.681s	15
14	**Kevin Magnussen**	McLaren	43 laps	4	1m34.242s	7
15	**Romain Grosjean**	Lotus	43 laps	5	1m35.984s	16
16	**Pastor Maldonado**	Lotus	43 laps	4	1m35.917s	22*
17	**Marcus Ericsson**	Caterham	43 laps	4	1m36.813s	17
18	**Max Chilton**	Marussia	43 laps	3	1m37.481s	21
19	**Kamui Kobyashi**	Caterham	43 laps	5	1m37.015s	19
20	**Jules Bianchi**	Marussia	41 laps/accident	3	1m37.015s	18
21	**Adrian Sutil**	Sauber	40 laps/accident	4	1m35.364s	14
R	**Fernando Alonso**	Ferrari	2 laps/electrical	0	1m33.740s	5

FASTEST LAP: : HAMILTON, 1M51.600S, 85.172MPH/137.071KPH ON LAP 39 • RACE LEADERS: ROSBERG 1-12, 15-28; HAMILTON 13-14, 29-44.
* 10-PLACE GRID PENALTY

RUSSIAN GP

A bold move into the first corner looked to have done the trick for Nico Rosberg, but he locked up as he passed Lewis Hamilton and flat-spotted his tyres, going from hero to zero and leaving Hamilton to win as he pleased.

The inaugural Russian GP should have been full of excitement, yet there was a sombre mood as drivers thought of Jules Bianchi, who had been so gravely injured at Suzuka.

Mercedes led the way again in qualifying, with Lewis Hamilton taking pole, and Valtteri Bottas and Jenson Button on the second row.

At the start, Nico Rosberg was the faster away and made a move for the lead down the inside into the second corner. It looked as though it was going to work too, but then he locked up and flat-spotted his tyres, necessitating an immediate pitstop and dropping him last but one place. Only Felipe Massa was further back, after starting down in 18th because of a fuel pump fault in qualifying. The Brazilian elected to take one of his two planned pitstops and charge from there, but he was to be thwarted by spending lap after lap stuck behind Sergio Perez's slower Force India on a circuit that didn't offer many opportunities for passing.

Hamilton thus had an easy run to his ninth win of 2014, as Bottas was never able to challenge him. Indeed, such was Mercedes's advantage that Rosberg was able to fight his way back through the order all the way through to his starting position, second. The team's ninth maximum score in 16 rounds was enough for it to land its first constructors' championship honours.

Button was delighted with fourth place and McLaren pleased as team-mate Kevin Magnussen's fifth place finish moved the team into fifth place in the rankings.

Neither Ferrari nor Red Bull Racing were on form in Sochi and Fernando Alonso had to make do with sixth, just 1.8s clear of Daniel Riccardo, in an afternoon that was ruined for the Spaniard when his front jack failed at his pitstop, costing him two positions. Alonso's other disappointment was that the F14 T's straightline speed was poor. The highest speed achieved through the speed trap in qualifying was 206.7mph by Williams, with Ferrari's best being 5.22mph slower.

SOCHI ROUND 16

DATE: **12 OCTOBER 2014**

Laps: **53** • Distance: **192.602 miles/309.963km** • Weather: **Sunny & warm**

Pos	Driver	Team	Result	Stops	Qualifying Time	Grid
1	**Lewis Hamilton**	Mercedes	1h31m50.744s	1	1m38.513s	1
2	**Nico Rosberg**	Mercedes	1h32m04.401s	1	1m38.713s	2
3	**Valtteri Bottas**	Williams	1h32m08.169s	1	1m38.920s	3
4	**Jenson Button**	McLaren	1h32m20.978s	1	1m39.121s	4
5	**Kevin Magnussen**	McLaren	1h32m44.360s	1	1m39.629s	11*
6	**Fernando Alonso**	Ferrari	1h32m50.760s	1	1m39.709s	7
7	**Daniel Ricciardo**	Red Bull	1h32m52.556s	1	1m39.635s	6
8	**Sebastian Vettel**	Red Bull	1h32m56.929s	1	1m40.052s	10
9	**Kimi Raikkonen**	Ferrari	1h33m09.621s	1	1m39.771s	8
10	**Sergio Perez**	Force India	1h33m10.811s	1	1m40.163s	12
11	**Felipe Massa**	Williams	1h33m11.621s	2	1m43.064s	18
12	**Nico Hulkenberg**	Force India	1h33m12.053s	1	1m40.058s	17*
13	**Jean-Eric Vergne**	Toro Rosso	1h33m28.039s	1	1m40.020s	9
14	**Daniil Kvyat**	Toro Rosso	52 laps	2	1m39.277s	5
15	**Esteban Gutierrez**	Sauber	52 laps	1	1m40.536s	13
16	**Adrian Sutil**	Sauber	52 laps	1	1m40.984s	14
17	**Romain Grosjean**	Lotus	52 laps	1	1m41.397s	15
18	**Pastor Maldonado**	Lotus	52 laps	1	1m43.205s	21*
19	**Marcus Ericsson**	Caterham	51 laps	2	1m42.648s	16
R	**Kamui Kobayashi**	Caterham	21 laps/brakes	0	1m43.166s	19
R	**Max Chilton**	Marussia	9 laps/suspension	1	1m43.649s	20*

FASTEST LAP: BOTTAS, 1M40.896S, 129.660MPH/208.668KPH ON LAP 53 • **RACE LEADERS:** HAMILTON 1-53
* 5-PLACE GRID PENALTY

Nico Rosberg took the lead from Hamilton at Turn 2, but this lock-up would ruin his race.

Russia's first taste of the World Championship was an event packed with colour in the very heart of the Black Sea resort Sochi.

When Nico Rosberg led away from pole, it looked as though he would cut a chunk out of Lewis Hamilton's points lead, but then Hamilton passed him midrace with a bold move and pulled clear for his 10th win of 2014.

Brake problems and a flatspotted tyre had spoiled Hamilton's qualifying session and left Rosberg dominant on pole. The German then got away well while Hamilton struggled for traction on the dirty side of the track, but was able to beat Valtteri Bottas to Turn 1. The order was then stabilized as the safety car was deployed – Sergio Perez had clattered into Adrian Sutil's Sauber at Turn 15. Not only did this take out both cars but it caused Sebastian Vettel to pit as he ran over some debris and his Red Bull suffered a puncture.

Rosberg appeared to be in control, but Hamilton began to attack after they emerged from their first pitstops, reducing the gap between them from 2.4s before catching Rosberg by surprise by diving down his inside from way back into Turn 12 on lap 24. After that, Rosberg had no response and their order was settled.

A slow second pitstop hampered Felipe Massa's run and allowed Daniel Ricciardo to sneak by to take the final spot on the podium. Of consolation to the Brazilian, he did at least beat his team-mate Bottas.

There was some battling behind them as Jenson Button tried to resist Fernando Alonso and failed, with Vettel then closing in on the Spaniard after a good drive from the tail of the field that included a fourth pitstop for fresh rubber just eight laps from the end. Kevin Magnussen also had to pit at the end of lap 1, also after running over debris, and he worked his way up the order too, to finish right on Vettel's tail.

Both Jean-Eric Vergne and Pastor Maldonado were hit with 5s penalties, with the Frenchman's being added to his race time, thus dropping him behind the Venezuelan, back to 10th.

The victory, his 32nd, made Hamilton the most successful British driver of all time. It also left him 24 points clear of Rosberg with two races to go, but there remained the possibility of the double-points final round upsetting his plans.

Hamilton hunted down and passed Rosberg to go on to a crucial win that gave him a 24-point lead.

CIRCUIT OF THE AMERICAS ROUND 17 DATE: 2 NOVEMBER
2014 Laps: **56** • Distance: **191.912 miles/308.853km** • Weather: **Sunny & warm**

Pos	Driver	Team	Result	Stops	Qualifying Time	Grid
1	**Lewis Hamilton**	Mercedes	1h40m04.785s	2	1m36.443s	2
2	**Nico Rosberg**	Mercedes	1h40m09.099s	2	1m36.067s	1
3	**Daniel Ricciardo**	Red Bull	1h40m30.345s	2	1m37.244s	5
4	**Felipe Massa**	Williams	1h40m31.709s	2	1m37.205s	4
5	**Valtteri Bottas**	Williams	1h40m35.777s	2	1m36.906s	3
6	**Fernando Alonso**	Ferrari	1h41m40.016s	2	1m37.610s	6
7	**Sebastian Vettel**	Red Bull	1h41m40.519s	4	1m39.621s	18!
8	**Kevin Magnussen**	McLaren	1h41m45.467s	2	1m37.706s	7
9	**Pastor Maldonado**	Lotus	1h41m52.655s	2	1m38.467s	10
10	**Jean-Eric Vergne**	Toro Rosso	1h41m53.648s	2	1m39.250s	14
11	**Romain Grosjean**	Lotus	55 laps	2	1m39.679s	16
12	**Jenson Button**	McLaren	55 laps	2	1m37.655s	12*
13	**Kimi Raikkonen**	Ferrari	55 laps	3	1m37.804s	8
14	**Esteban Gutierrez**	Sauber	55 laps	3	1m39.555s	15
15	**Daniil Kvyat**	Toro Rosso	55 laps	3	1m38.699s	17**
R	**Nico Hulkenberg**	Force India	16 laps/power unit	1	1m38.598s	13
R	**Sergio Perez**	Force India	1 lap/Accident damage	0	1m38.554s	11
R	**Adrian Sutil**	Sauber	0 laps/Accident	0	1m38.810s	9

FASTEST LAP: VETTEL, 1M41.379S, 121.644MPH/195.767KPH ON LAP 50 • RACE LEADERS: ROSBERG 1-15, 17-23, 3; HAMILTON 16, 24-33, 35-56
* 5-PLACE GRID PENALTY ** 10-PLACE GRID PENALTY
! TO START FROM PITLANE FOR USING SIXTH POWER UNIT OF SEASON

BRAZILIAN GP

Lewis Hamilton looked set to topple Nico Rosberg, but he pushed too hard, half spun and so let his team-mate off the hook and enabled him to close the gap between them to 17 points with one race to run.

The battle for pole position was as close as ever and, for the third time in four rounds, it was Nico Rosberg who grabbed the prime spot, this time with Lewis Hamilton just 0.033s slower. This was duly converted into the lead, so the German had achieved his first target for race day, knowing that he had to grab every advantage in his pursuit of the victory that was all but essential if he wanted to become World Champion.

Hamilton tucked in behind him and stayed there, determined not to let it slip as he did the weekend before outside Austin.

The Mercedes made early first pitstops that indicated that they would be coming in three times. And it was at the second of these visits that the race hinged. As race leader, Rosberg was called in first, on lap 26. Having been instructed to "push", Hamilton presumed that he would be brought in next time around, so he took every last fraction of grip out of his tyres, only to find that the team wanted him to stay out for one further lap. It was on this lap that his result was decided as he made a mistake and half spun at Descida do Lago. The delay denied him the chance to come out of his stop in front. Despite a concerted charge on his third set of tyres, on which he closed onto Rosberg's tail again, his opportunity had gone.

The third driver to finish on the podium, Felipe Massa, also made a mistake. He pulled in to the wrong pit for his second tyre change, having mistaken the McLaren mechanics' pale overalls with the ones worn by his Williams pit crew. At least it didn't cost him a position. Had it done so, he would have handed it to Jenson Button, who put on a defiantly strong drive as McLaren seemed to be easing him towards the exit to make way for Fernando Alonso being the team leader in 2015. That his team-mate Kevin Magnussen could finish only ninth after suffering tyre degradation made the likelihood of the young Dane staying on seem all the more perplexing.

INTERLAGOS ROUND 18

DATE: **9 NOVEMBER 2014**

Laps: **60** • Distance: **188.749 miles/303.763km** • Weather: **Hot & humid**

Pos	Driver	Team	Result	Stops	Qualifying Time	Grid
1	**Nico Rosberg**	Mercedes	1h30m02.555s	3	1m10.023s	1
2	**Lewis Hamilton**	Mercedes	1h30m04.012s	3	1m10.056s	2
3	**Felipe Massa**	Williams	1h30m43.586s	3	1m10.247s	3
4	**Jenson Button**	McLaren	1h30m51.213s	3	1m10.930s	5
5	**Sebastian Vettel**	Red Bull	1h30m53.975s	3	1m10.938s	6
6	**Fernando Alonso**	Ferrari	1h31m04.461s	3	1m10.977s	8
7	**Kimi Raikkonen**	Ferrari	1h31m06.285s	2	1m11.099s	10
8	**Nico Hulkenberg**	Force India	1h31m06.409s	3	1m11.976s	12
9	**Kevin Magnussen**	McLaren	1h31m12.640s	3	1m10.969s	7
10	**Valtteri Bottas**	Williams	70 laps	3	1m10.305s	4
11	**Daniil Kvyat**	Toro Rosso	70 laps	3	no time	17*
12	**Pastor Maldonado**	Lotus	70 laps	3	1m12.233s	16
13	**Jean-Eric Vergne**	Toro Rosso	70 laps	3	1m12.040s	15
14	**Esteban Gutierrez**	Sauber	70 laps	3	1m11.591s	11
15	**Sergio Perez**	Force India	70 laps	3	1m12.076s	18*
16	**Adrian Sutil**	Sauber	70 laps	3	1m12.099s	13
17	**Romain Grosjean**	Lotus	63 laps/power unit	3	1m12.037s	14
R	**Daniel Ricciardo**	Red Bull	39 laps/suspension	2	1m11.075s	9

FASTEST LAP: HAMILTON, 1M13.555S, 131.044MPH/210.895KPH ON LAP 62 • RACE LEADERS: ROSBERG 1–6, 14–25, 29–49, 52–71; HAMILTON 7–8, 26–28, 50–51; HULKENBERG 9–13
* 7-PLACE GRID PENALTY

Rosberg celebrates taking the win while Massa revels in being on the podium for his home race.

Hamilton knew that second would ensure him his second F1 title, but he powered ahead of rival Rosberg and then knew the title was his when his team-mate's Mercedes was slowed, letting him win both the day and the year.

Helped by starting on the side of the grid that had been in the sun more recently, Lewis Hamilton made the most of the extra grip and produced what he thought was his best start ever, being well clear long before they had reached the first corner.

This made his life easier and it was now up to team-mate and title rival Nico Rosberg to respond. Yet their first of two planned pitstops came and went and there was no change of position. Things were definitely going the Englishman's way and then, at mid-distance, things became a whole lot better for him as Rosberg followed an off-track moment with a slow lap and then more off-track moments. His Mercedes's ERS had failed, due to overheating, and this was robbing him of the 160bhp provision that he could otherwise use for 33s of each lap. Down the order he tumbled, with increasingly plaintive radio messages asking what could be done to fix it. Nothing it seems, and he fell first out of title reckoning, then out of the points.

Hamilton wasn't too interested in now racing to victory, wary lest his car hit similar problems. Instead, he was happy to cruise and collect, but his team urged him on as Felipe Massa began to close in with a strong final stint on the super-soft tyres. But he did enough and so claimed his 11th win of the year before being overcome emotionally when he reached the privacy of the waiting room behind the podium. He had done it, becoming Britain's first F1 double champion since Jackie Stewart achieved the feat in 1971.

Massa completed a Williams two-three finish, but perhaps the drive of the race came from Daniel Ricciardo who, like Red Bull team-mate Sebastian Vettel, had to start from the pitlane after his Red Bull RTB10's front wings were found to be flexing too much. Even so, he raced through to fourth to cap a great first year with the team.

There was a big gap back to Jenson Button in fifth, with Nico Hulkenberg closing in fast behind.

A remarkable start from second on the grid put Hamilton into a lead that let him control the race.

YAS MARINA ROUND 19

DATE: **23 NOVEMBER 2014**

Laps: **55** • Distance: **189.805 miles/305.462km** • Weather: **Hot & dry**

Pos	Driver	Team	Result	Stops	Qualifying Time	Grid
1	Lewis Hamilton	Mercedes	1h39m02.619s	2	1m40.866s	2
2	Felipe Massa	Williams	1h39m05.195s	2	1m41.119s	4
3	Valtteri Bottas	Williams	1h39m31.499s	2	1m41.025s	3
4	Daniel Ricciardo	Red Bull	1h39m39.856s	2	No time	20*
5	Jenson Button	McLaren	1h40m02.953s	2	1m41.964s	6
6	Nico Hulkenberg	Force India	1h40m04.767s	2	1m42.384s	12
7	Sergio Perez	Force India	1h40m13.679s	2	1m42.239s	11
8	Sebastian Vettel	Red Bull	1h40m14.664s	2	No time	19*
9	Fernando Alonso	Ferrari	1h40m28.432s	2	1m42.866s	8
10	Kimi Raikkonen	Ferrari	1h40m30.439s	2	1m42.236s	7
11	Kevin Magnussen	McLaren	1h40m32.995s	2	1m42.198s	9
12	Jean-Eric Vergne	Toro Rosso	1h40m34.566s	3	1m42.207s	10
13	Romain Grosjean	Lotus	54 laps	3	1m42.768s	18**
14	Nico Rosberg	Mercedes	54 laps	2	1m40.480s	1
15	Esteban Gutierrez	Sauber	54 laps	2	1m42.819s	14
16	Adrian Sutil	Sauber	54 laps	3	1m43.074s	13
17	Will Stevens	Caterham	54 laps	2	1m45.095s	17
R	Kamui Kobayashi	Caterham	42 laps/vibration	2	1m44.540s	16
R	Pastor Maldonado	Lotus	26 laps/engine	1	1m42.860s	15
R	Daniil Kvyat	Toro Rosso	14 laps/engine	1	1m41.908s	5

FASTEST LAP: RICCIARDO, 1M44.496S, 118.894MPH/191.341KPH ON LAP 50 • RACE LEADERS: HAMILTON 1-10, 14-31 & 44-55; ROSBERG 11; MASSA 12-13, 32-43
* EXCLUDED FROM QULAIFYING, STARTED FROM PITLANE
**20-PLACE GRID PENALTY

Lewis Hamilton celebrates becoming Formula 1 World Champion for the second time. The Mercedes driver became only the fourth British multiple winner after Graham Hill (1962 & 1968), Jim Clark (1963 & 1965) and Jackie Stewart (1969, 1971 & 1973).

POS	DRIVER	NAT		CAR-ENGINE	R1	R2	R3	R4	R5
1	LEWIS HAMILTON	GBR		MERCEDES F1 W05	RP	1PF	1	1P	1P
2	NICO ROSBERG	GER		MERCEDES F1 W05	1F	2	2PF	2F	2
3	DANIEL RICCIARDO	AUS		RED BULL-RENAULT RB10	D	R	4	4	3
4	VALTTERI BOTTAS	FIN		WILLIAMS-MERCEDES FW36	5	8	8	7	5
5	SEBASTIAN VETTEL	GER		RED BULL-RENAULT RB10	R	3	6	5	4F
6	FERNANDO ALONSO	SPA		FERRARI F14 T	4	4	9	3	6
7	FELIPE MASSA	BRA		WILLIAMS-MERCEDES FW36	R	7	7	15	13
8	JENSON BUTTON	GBR		McLAREN-MERCEDES MP4-29	3	6	17	11	11
9	NICO HULKENBERG	GER		FORCE INDIA-MERCEDES VJM07	6	5	5	6	10
10	SERGIO PEREZ	MEX		FORCE INDIA-MERCEDES VJM07	10	NS	3	9	9
11	KEVIN MAGNUSSEN	DEN		McLAREN-MERCEDES MP4-29	2	9	R	13	12
12	KIMI RAIKKONEN	FIN		FERRARI F14 T	7	12	10	8	7
13	JEAN-ERIC VERGNE	FRA		TORO ROSSO-RENAULT STR9	8	R	R	12	R
14	ROMAIN GROSJEAN	FRA		LOTUS-RENAULT E22	R	11	12	R	8
15	DANIIL KYVAT	RUS		TORO ROSSO-RENAULT STR9	9	10	11	10	14
16	PASTOR MALDONADO	VEN		LOTUS-RENAULT E22	R	R	14	14	15
17	JULES BIANCHI	FRA		MARUSSIA-FERRARI MR03	NC	R	16	17	18
18	ADRIAN SUTIL	GER		SAUBER-FERRARI C33	11	R	R	R	17
19	MARCUS ERICSSON	SWE		CATERHAM-RENAULT CT05	R	14	R	20	20
20	ESTEBAN GUTIERREZ	MEX		SAUBER-FERRARI C33	12	R	R	16	16
21	MAX CHILTON	GBR		MARUSSIA-FERRARI MR03	13	15	13	19	19
22	KAMUI KOBAYASHI	JPN		CATERHAM-RENAULT CT05	R	13	15	18	R
23	WILL STEVENS	GBR		CATERHAM-RENAULT CT05	-	-	-	-	-
24	ANDRE LOTTERER	GER		CATERHAM-RENAULT CT05	-	-	-	-	-

SCORING

1st	25 points
2nd	18 points
3rd	15 points
4th	12 points
5th	10 points
6th	8 points
7th	6 points
8th	4 points
9th	2 points
10th	1 point

 Double points allocation for final round

POS	TEAM-ENGINE	R1	R2	R3	R4	R5
1	MERCEDES	1/R	1/2	1/2	1/2	1/2
2	RED BULL-RENAULT	D/R	3/R	4/6	4/5	3/4
3	WILLIAMS-MERCEDES	5/R	7/8	7/8	7/15	5/13
4	FERRARI	4/7	4/12	9/10	3/8	6/7
5	McLAREN-MERCEDES	2/3	6/9	17/R	11/13	11/12
6	FORCE INDIA-MERCEDES	6/10	5/NS	3/5	6/9	9/10
7	TORO ROSSO-RENAULT	8/9	10/R	11/R	10/12	14/R
8	LOTUS-RENAULT	R/R	11/R	12/14	14/R	8/15
9	MARUSSIA-FERRARI	13/NC	15/R	13/16	17/19	18/19
10	SAUBER-FERRARI	11/12	R/R	R/R	16/R	16/17
11	CATERHAM-RENAULT	R/R	13/14	15/R	18/20	20/R

SYMBOLS AND GRAND PRIX KEY

ROUND 1................. AUSTRALIAN GP
ROUND 2.................MALAYSIAN GP
ROUND 3..................... BAHRAIN GP
ROUND 4..................... CHINESE GP
ROUND 5..................... SPANISH GP

ROUND 6..................... MONACO GP
ROUND 7................... CANADIAN GP
ROUND 8..................... AUSTRIAN GP
ROUND 9..................... BRITISH GP
ROUND 10 .... GERMAN GP

ROUND 11 .... HUNGARIAN GP
ROUND 12 .... BELGIAN GP
ROUND 13 .... ITALIAN GP
ROUND 14 ....SINGAPORE GP
ROUND 15.................JAPANESE GP

ROUND 16 .... RUSSIAN GP
ROUND 17.......... UNITED STATES GP
ROUND 18 .... BRAZILIAN GP
ROUND 19 ....ABU DHABI GP*

D DISQUALIFIED   **F** FASTEST LAP   **NC** NOT CLASSIFIED   **NS** NON-STARTER   **P** POLE POSITION   **R** RETIRED   **W** WITHDRAWN

R6	R7	R8	R9	R10	R11	R12	R13	R14	R15	R16	R17	R18	R19	TOTAL
2	R	2	1F	3F	3	R	1PF	1PF	1F	1P	1	2F	1	384
1P	2P	1	RP	1P	4PF	2PF	2	R	2P	2	2P	1P	14P	317
3	1	8	3	6	1	1	5	3	4	7	3	R	4F	238
R	7	3	2	2	8	3	4	11	6	3F	5	10	3	186
R	3	R	5	4	7	5	6	2	3	8	7F	5	8	167
4	6	5	6	5	2	7	R	4	R	6	6	6	9	161
7	12F	4P	R	R	5	13	3	5	7	11	4	3	2	134
6	4	11	4	8	10	6	8	R	5	4	12	4	5	126
5	5	9	8	7	R	10	12	9	8	12	R	8	6	96
R	11	6F	11	10	R	8	7	7	10	10	R	15	7	59
10	9	7	7	9	12	12	10	10	14	5	8	9	11	55
12F	10	10	R	11	6	4	9	8	12	9	13	7	10	55
R	8	R	10	13	9	11	13	6	9	13	10	13	12	22
8	R	14	12	R	R	R	16	13	15	17	11	17	13	8
R	R	R	9	R	14	9	11	14	11	14	15	11	R	8
NS	R	12	17	12	13	R	14	12	16	18	9	12	R	2
9	R	15	14	15	15	18	18	16	20	-	-	-	-	2
R	13	13	13	R	11	14	15	R	21	16	R	16	16	0
11	R	18	R	18	R	17	20	15	17	19	-	-	-	0
R	14	19	R	14	R	15	19	R	13	15	14	14	15	0
14	R	17	16	17	16	16	R	17	18	R	-	-	-	0
13	R	16	15	16	R	-	17	R	19	R	-	-	R	0
-	-	-	-	-	-	-	-	-	-	-	-	-	17	0
-	-	-	-	-	-	R	-	-	-	-	-	-	-	0

R6	R7	R8	R9	R10	R11	R12	R13	R14	R15	R16	R17	R18	R19	TOTAL
1/2	2/R	1/2	1/R	1/3	3/4	2/R	1/2	1/R	1/2	1/2	1/2	1/2	1/14	701
3/R	1/3	8/R	3/5	4/6	1/7	1/5	5/6	2/3	3/4	7/8	3/7	5/R	4/8	405
7/R	7/12	3/4	2/R	2/R	5/8	3/13	3/4	5/11	6/7	3/11	4/5	3/10	2/3	320
4/12	6/10	5/10	6/R	5/11	2/6	4/7	9/R	4/8	12/R	6/9	6/13	6/7	9/10	216
6/10	4/9	7/11	4/7	8/9	10/12	6/12	8/10	10/R	5/14	4/5	8/12	4/9	5/11	181
5/R	5/11	6/9	8/11	7/10	R/R	8/10	7/12	7/9	8/10	10/12	R/r	8/15	6/7	155
R/R	8/R	R/R	9/10	13/R	9/14	9/11	11/13	6/14	9/11	13/14	10/15	11/13	12/R	30
8/NS	R/R	12/14	12/17	12/R	13/R	R/R	14/16	12/13	15/16	17/18	9/11	12/17	13/R	10
9/14	R/R	15/17	14/16	15/17	15/16	16/18	18/R	16/17	18/20	R/-	-/-	-/-	-/-	2
R/R	13/14	13/19	13/R	14/R	11/R	14/15	15/19	R/R	13/21	15/16	14/R	14/16	15/16	0
11/13	R/R	16/18	15/R	16/18	R/R	17/R	17/20	15/R	17/19	19/R	-/-	-/-	17/R	0

117

FORMULA ONE RECORDS

MOST STARTS

DRIVERS

325	Rubens Barrichello	(BRA)
308	Michael Schumacher	(GER)
266	Jenson Button	(GBR)
256	Riccardo Patrese	(ITA)
	Jarno Trulli	(ITA)
247	David Coulthard	(GBR)
236	Fernando Alonso	(SPA)
230	Giancarlo Fisichella	(ITA)
216	Mark Webber	(AUS)
213	Kimi Raikkonen	(FIN)
211	Felipe Massa	(BRA)
210	Gerhard Berger	(AUT)
208	Andrea de Cesaris	(ITA)
204	Nelson Piquet	(BRA)
201	Jean Alesi	(FRA)
199	Alain Prost	(FRA)
194	Michele Alboreto	(ITA)
187	Nigel Mansell	(GBR)
185	Nick Heidfeld	(GER)
180	Ralf Schumacher	(GER)
176	Graham Hill	(GBR)
175	Jacques Laffite	(FRA)
171	Niki Lauda	(AUT)
166	Nico Rosberg	(GER)
165	Jacques Villeneuve	(CDN)
163	Thierry Boutsen	(BEL)
162	Mika Hakkinen	(FIN)
	Johnny Herbert	(GBR)

161	Ayrton Senna	(BRA)
159	Heinz-Harald Frentzen	(GER)
158	Martin Brundle	(GBR)
	Olivier Panis	(FRA)
152	John Watson	(GBR)
149	Rene Arnoux	(FRA)
148	Lewis Hamilton	(GBR)
147	Eddie Irvine	(GBR)
	Derek Warwick	(GBR)
146	Carlos Reutemann	(ARG)
144	Emerson Fittipaldi	(BRA)
139	Sebastian Vettel	(GER)
135	Jean-Pierre Jarier	(FRA)
132	Eddie Cheever	(USA)
	Clay Regazzoni	(SWI)
128	Mario Andretti	(USA)
126	Jack Brabham	(AUS)
123	Ronnie Peterson	(SWE)
119	Pierluigi Martini	(ITA)
116	Damon Hill	(GBR)
	Jacky Ickx	(BEL)
	Alan Jones	(AUS)
114	Keke Rosberg	(FIN)
	Patrick Tambay	(FRA)
112	Denny Hulme	(NZL)
	Jody Scheckter	(RSA

CONSTRUCTORS

889	Ferrari
762	McLaren
681	Williams
553	Lotus* (né Toleman, then Benetton, then Renault*)
507	Toro Rosso (né Minardi)
492	Lotus
418	Tyrrell
416	Force India (né Jordan, then Midland, then Spyker)
409	Prost (né Ligier)
394	Brabham
383	Arrows
	Sauber (including BMW Sauber)
319	Red Bull (né Stewart, then Jaguar Racing)
284	Mercedes GP (né BAR, then Honda Racing, then Brawn GP)
230	March
197	BRM
132	Osella
129	Renault

Jenson Button made the first of his 266 starts in Australia in 2000, for Williams. He retired from the race, as did Pedro Diniz following in a Sauber.

Michael Schumacher scored his 91st and final grand prix win when he led home his Ferrari team-mate Rubens Barrichello in the 2005 American GP.

MOST WINS

DRIVERS

91	Michael Schumacher	(GER)	**14**	Jack Brabham	(AUS)	**8**	Denny Hulme	(NZL)
51	Alain Prost	(FRA)		Emerson Fittipaldi	(BRA)		Jacky Ickx	(BEL)
41	Ayrton Senna	(BRA)		Graham Hill	(GBR)		Nico Rosberg	(GER)
39	Sebastian Vettel	(GER)	**13**	Alberto Ascari	(ITA)	**7**	Rene Arnoux	(FRA)
33	Lewis Hamilton	(GBR)		David Coulthard	(GBR)		Juan Pablo Montoya	(COL)
31	Nigel Mansell	(GBR)	**12**	Mario Andretti	(USA)	**6**	Tony Brooks	(GBR)
27	Jackie Stewart	(GBR)		Alan Jones	(AUS)		Jacques Laffite	(FRA)
25	Jim Clark	(GBR)		Carlos Reutemann	(ARG)		Riccardo Patrese	(ITA)
	Niki Lauda	(AUT)	**11**	Rubens Barrichello	(BRA)		Jochen Rindt	(AUT)
24	Juan Manuel Fangio	(ARG)		Felipe Massa	(BRA)		Ralf Schumacher	(GER)
23	Nelson Piquet	(BRA)		Jacques Villeneuve	(CDN)		John Surtees	(GBR)
22	Damon Hill	(GBR)	**10**	Gerhard Berger	(AUT)		Gilles Villeneuve	(CDN)
20	Mika Hakkinen	(FIN)		James Hunt	(GBR)			
	Kimi Raikkonen	(FIN)		Ronnie Peterson	(SWE)			
16	Stirling Moss	(GBR)		Jody Scheckter	(RSA)			
15	Jenson Button	(GBR)	**9**	Mark Webber	(AUS)			

CONSTRUCTORS

221	Ferrari	**16**	Cooper	**1**	BMW Sauber
181	McLaren	**15**	Renault		Eagle
114	Williams	**10**	Alfa Romeo		Hesketh
79	Lotus	**9**	Ligier		Penske
51	Red Bull (including Stewart)		Maserati		Porsche
49	Lotus* (including Benetton, Renault II)		Matra		Shadow
35	Brabham		Mercedes		Toro Rosso
29	Mercedes GP (including Honda Racing, Brawn GP)		Vanwall		
23	Tyrrell	**4**	Jordan		
17	BRM	**3**	March		
			Wolf		
		2	Honda		

Sebastian Vettel equalled Michael Schumacher's record of 13 wins in a season in 2013. Here he wins the tenth, in India, to clinch his fourth title.

DRIVERS

13	Sebastian Vettel	2013		Ayrton Senna	1988		Jenson Button	2009
	Michael Schumacher	2004	**7**	Fernando Alonso	2005		Jim Clark	1965
11	Lewis Hamilton	2014		Fernando Alonso	2006		Juan Manuel Fangio	1954
	Michael Schumacher	2002		Jim Clark	1963		Damon Hill	1994
	Sebastian Vettel	2011		Alain Prost	1984		James Hunt	1976
9	Nigel Mansell	1992		Alain Prost	1988		Nigel Mansell	1987
	Michael Schumacher	1995		Alain Prost	1993		Kimi Raikkonen	2007
	Michael Schumacher	2000		Kimi Raikkonen	2005		Michael Schumacher	1998
	Michael Schumacher	2001		Ayrton Senna	1991		Michael Schumacher	2003
8	Mika Hakkinen	1998		Jacques Villeneuve	1997		Michael Schumacher	2006
	Damon Hill	1996	**6**	Mario Andretti	1978		Ayrton Senna	1989
	Michael Schumacher	1994		Alberto Ascari	1952		Ayrton Senna	1990

CONSTRUCTORS

16	Mercedes GP	2014		Ferrari	2006		Williams	1997
15	Ferrari	2002		Ferrari	2007	**7**	Ferrari	1952
	Ferrari	2004		McLaren	1998		Ferrari	1953
	McLaren	1988		Red Bull	2010		Ferrari	2008
12	McLaren	1984		Williams	1986		Lotus	1963
	Red Bull	2011		Williams	1987		Lotus	1973
	Williams	1996	**8**	Benetton	1994		McLaren	1999
11	Benetton	1995		Brawn GP	2009		McLaren	2000
10	Ferrari	2000		Ferrari	2003		McLaren	2012
	McLaren	2005		Lotus	1978		Red Bull	2012
	McLaren	1989		McLaren	1991		Tyrrell	1971
	Williams	1992		McLaren	2007		Williams	1991
	Williams	1993		Renault	2005		Williams	1994
9	Ferrari	2001		Renault	2006			

MOST POLE POSITIONS

DRIVERS

68	Michael Schumacher	(GER)
65	Ayrton Senna	(BRA)
45	Sebastian Vettel	(GER)
38	Lewis Hamilton	(GBR)
33	Jim Clark	(GBR)
	Alain Prost	(FRA)
32	Nigel Mansell	(GBR)
29	Juan Manuel Fangio	(ARG)
26	Mika Hakkinen	(FIN)
24	Niki Lauda	(AUT)
	Nelson Piquet	(BRA)
22	Fernando Alonso	(SPA)
20	Damon Hill	(GBR)
18	Mario Andretti	(USA)
	Rene Arnoux	(FRA)
17	Jackie Stewart	(GBR)
16	Felipe Massa	(BRA)
	Stirling Moss	(GBR)
	Kimi Raikkonen	(FIN)
15	Nico Rosberg	(GER)
14	Alberto Ascari	(ITA)
	Rubens Barrichello	(BRA)
	James Hunt	(GBR)
	Ronnie Peterson	(SWE)
13	Jack Brabham	(AUS)
	Graham Hill	(GBR)
	Jacky Ickx	(BEL)
	Juan Pablo Montoya	(COL)
	Jacques Villeneuve	(CDN)
12	Gerhard Berger	(AUT)
	David Coulthard	(GBR)
11	Mark Webber	(AUS)
10	Jochen Rindt	(AUT)

CONSTRUCTORS

207	Ferrari
154	McLaren
128	Williams
107	Lotus
58	Red Bull
39	Brabham
35	Mercedes GP (including Brawn GP, Honda Racing, BAR)
34	Lotus* (including Toleman, Benetton, Renault II)
31	Renault
14	Tyrrell
12	Alfa Romeo
11	BRM
	Cooper
10	Maserati
9	Ligier
8	Mercedes
7	Vanwall
5	March
4	Matra
3	Force India (including Jordan)
	Shadow
	Toyota
2	Lancia
1	BMW Sauber
	Toro Rosso

Nigel Mansell claimed one of his 14 poles in 1992 for Williams at Estoril.

FASTEST LAPS

DRIVERS

76	Michael Schumacher	(GER)
41	Alain Prost	(FRA)
40	Kimi Raikkonen	(FIN)
30	Nigel Mansell	(GBR)
28	Jim Clark	(GBR)
25	Mika Hakkinen	(FIN)
24	Niki Lauda	(AUT)
	Sebastian Vettel	(GER)
23	Juan Manuel Fangio	(ARG)
	Nelson Piquet	(BRA)
21	Fernando Alonso	(SPA)
	Gerhard Berger	(AUT)
20	Lewis Hamilton	(GBR)
19	Damon Hil	(GBR)
	Stirling Moss	(GBR)
	Ayrton Senna	(BRA)
	Mark Webber	(AUS)
18	David Coulthard	(GBR)
17	Rubens Barrichello	(BRA)
16	Felipe Massa	(BRA)
15	Clay Regazzoni	(SWI)
	Jackie Stewart	(GBR)
14	Jacky Ickx	(BEL)
13	Alberto Ascari	(ITA)
	Alan Jones	(AUS)
	Riccardo Patrese	(ITA)
12	Rene Arnoux	(FRA)
	Jack Brabham	(AUS)
	Juan Pablo Montoya	(COL)
11	John Surtees	(GBR)

CONSTRUCTORS

228	Ferrari
152	McLaren
133	Williams
71	Lotus
54	Lotus* (including Toleman, Benetton, Renault II)
44	Red Bull
40	Brabham
22	Tyrrell
19	Mercedes GP
18	Renault
15	BRM
	Maserati
14	Alfa Romeo
13	Cooper
12	Matra
11	Prost (including Ligier)
7	March
6	Vanwall

MOST POINTS (THIS FIGURE IS GROSS TALLY, I.E. INCLUDING SCORES THAT WERE LATER DROPPED)

DRIVERS

1618	Sebastian Vettel	(GER)
1606	Fernando Alonso	(SPA)
1566	Michael Schumacher	(GER)
1486	Lewis Hamilton	(GBR)
1198	Jenson Button	(GBR)
1047.5	Mark Webber	(AUS)
1024	Kimi Raikkonen	(FIN)
950	Felipe Massa	(BRA)
887.5	Nico Rosberg	(GER)
798.5	Alain Prost	(FRA)
658	Rubens Barrichello	(BRA)
614	Ayrton Senna	(BRA)
535	David Coulthard	(GBR)
485.5	Nelson Piquet	(BRA)
482	Nigel Mansell	(GBR)
420.5	Niki Lauda	(AUT)
420	Mika Hakkinen	(FIN)
385	Gerhard Berger	(AUT)
360	Damon Hill	(GBR)
	Jackie Stewart	(GBR)
329	Ralf Schumacher	(GER)
310	Carlos Reutemann	(ARG)
307	Juan Pablo Montoya	(COL)
289	Graham Hill	(GBR)
281	Emerson Fittipaldi	(BRA)
	Riccardo Patrese	(ITA)
277.5	Juan Manuel Fangio	(ARG)
275	Giancarlo Fisichella	(ITA)
274	Jim Clark	(GBR)
273	Robert Kubica	(POL)
268	Daniel Ricciardo	(AUS)
261	Jack Brabham	(AUS)
259	Nick Heidfeld	(GER)
255	Jody Scheckter	(RSA)
248	Denny Hulme	(NZL)
246.5	Jarno Trulli	(ITA)

CONSTRUCTORS

5600.5	Ferrari
4990.5	McLaren
3081	Williams
2953.5	Red Bull (including Stewart, Jaguar Racing)
2467.5	Lotus* (including Toleman, Benetton, Renault II)
2085	Mercedes GP (including BAR, Honda Racing, Brawn GP)
1514	Lotus
854	Brabham
783	Force India (including Jordan, Midland, Spyker)
767	Sauber (including BMW Sauber)
617	Tyrrell
439	BRM
424	Prost (including Ligier)
333	Cooper
312	Renault
278.5	Toyota
237	Toro Rosso
171.5	March
167	Arrows
155	Matra

Not every team can score points every year: despite Adrian Sutil's best efforts, Sauber failed to add to its all-time tally of 767 points in 2014.

MOST DRIVERS' TITLES

7	Michael Schumacher	(GER)	Jim Clark	(GBR)	Denis Hulme	(NZL)	
5	Juan Manuel Fangio	(ARG)	Emerson Fittipaldi	(BRA)	James Hunt	(GBR)	
4	Alain Prost	(FRA)	Mika Hakkinen	(FIN)	Alan Jones	(AUS)	
	Sebastian Vettel	(GER)	Lewis Hamilton	(GBR)	Nigel Mansell	(GBR)	
3	Jack Brabham	(AUS)	Graham Hill	(GBR)	Kimi Raikkonen	(FIN)	
	Niki Lauda	(AUT)	**1** Mario Andretti	(USA)	Jochen Rindt	(AUT)	
	Nelson Piquet	(BRA)	Jenson Button	(GBR)	Keke Rosberg	(FIN)	
	Ayrton Senna	(BRA)	Giuseppe Farina	(ITA)	Jody Scheckter	(RSA)	
	Jackie Stewart	(GBR)	Mike Hawthorn	(GBR)	John Surtees	(GBR)	
2	Fernando Alonso	(SPA)	Damon Hill	(GBR)	Jacques Villeneuve	(CDN)	
	Alberto Ascari	(ITA)	Phil Hill	(USA)			

MOST CONSTRUCTORS' TITLES

16	Ferrari	**2**	Brabham		BRM
9	Williams		Cooper		Matra
8	McLaren		Renault		Mercedes GP
7	Lotus	**1**	Benetton		Tyrrell
4	Red Bull		Brawn		Vanwall

NB. To avoid confusion, the Lotus stats listed are based on the team that ran from 1958 to 1994, whereas the those listed as Lotus* are for the team based at Enstone, which started as Toleman in 1981, became Benetton in 1986, then Renault II in 2002 and Lotus in 2012. The Renault listings are for the team that ran from 1977 to 1985; the stats for Red Bull Racing include those of the Stewart Grand Prix and Jaguar Racing teams from which it evolved, and those for Mercedes GP for the team that started as BAR in 1999, then ran as Honda GP from 2006 and as Brawn GP in 2009. Force India's stats include those of Jordan, Midland and Spyker, while Scuderia Toro Rosso's include those of its forerunner Minardi

2015 FILL-IN CHART

	DRIVER	TEAM	Round 1 – 15 March AUSTRALIAN GP	Round 2 – 29 March MALAYSIAN GP	Round 3 – 12 April CHINESE GP	Round 4 – 19 April BAHRAIN GP	Round 5 – 10 May SPANISH GP	Round 6 – 24 May MONACO GP	Round 7 – 7 June CANADIAN GP	Round 8 – 21 June AUSTRIAN GP
44	LEWIS HAMILTON	Mercedes								
6	NICO ROSBERG	Mercedes								
3	DANIEL RICCIARDO	Red Bull								
26	DANIIL KVYAT	Red Bull								
19	FELIPE MASSA	Williams								
77	VALTTERI BOTTAS	Williams								
5	SEBASTIAN VETTEL	Ferrari								
7	KIMI RAIKKONEN	Ferrari								
14	FERNANDO ALONSO	McLaren								
22	JENSON BUTTON	McLaren								
11	SERGIO PEREZ	Force India								
27	NICO HULKENBERG	Force India								
55	CARLOS SAINZ JR	Toro Rosso								
33	MAX VERSTAPPEN	Toro Rosso								
8	ROMAIN GROSJEAN	Lotus								
13	PASTOR MALDONADO	Lotus								
9	MARCUS ERICSSON	Sauber								
12	FELIPE NASR	Sauber								

124

SCORING SYSTEM: 25, 18, 15, 12, 10, 8, 6, 4, 2, 1 POINTS
FOR THE FIRST 10 FINISHERS IN EACH GRAND PRIX

Round 9 – 5 July BRITISH GP	Round 10 – 19 July GERMAN GP	Round 11 – 26 July HUNGARIAN GP	Round 12 – 23 Aug BELGIAN GP	Round 13 – 6 Sep ITALIAN GP	Round 14 – 20 Sep SINGAPORE GP	Round 15 – 27 Sep JAPANESE GP	Round 16 – 11 Oct RUSSIAN GP	Round 17 – 25 Oct UNITED STATES GP	Round 18 – 1 Nov MEXICAN GP	Round 19 – 15 Nov BRAZILIAN GP	Round 20 – 29 Nov ABU DHABI GP	POINTS TOTAL

The World Championship remains a televisual delight. This is Romain Grosjean pressing on through the dark at the Marina Bay Circuit.

From the first test to the last race, every departure from the pit garage has a purpose in the quest to be top.

The publishers would like to thank the following sources for their kind permission to reproduce the pictures in this book.

Getty Images: /Mark Thompson: 61B

LAT Photographic: 21, 27, 33, 37, 47, 63T, 63R, 63B, 118, 119, 121; /Lorenzo Bellanca: 61TL; /Sam Bloxham: 5, 55, 56-57, 82-83, 104; /Charles Coates: 14-15, 19, 29, 39, 40-41, 44, 50-51, 53, 54, 59BL, 63L, 103, 106, 108-109, 110, 114-115, 120, 121; /Glenn Dunbar: 11, 18, 22, 23, 24-25, 36, 90-91, 93, 96, 102; /Steve Etherington: 12, 64-65, 66-67, 92, 98, 107, 112, 128; /Andrew Ferraro: 43, 59BR; / Andrew Hone: 3, 17, 26, 59T, 95, 97, 105, 111, 113, 126-127; /Sebastiaan Rozendaal/Dutch Photo Agency: 45; /Alastair Staley: 6-7, 10, 13, 28, 32, 34, 38, 42, 46, 48, 49, 52, 94, 100, 101; /Steven Tee: 8-9, 16, 20, 30-31, 35, 99; /Mark Thompson/Getty Images/Red Bull Racing: 61TR

Every effort has been made to acknowledge correctly and contact the source and/or copyright holder of each picture and Carlton Books Limited apologizes for any unintentional errors or omissions that will be corrected in future editions of this book.